What
Babies
Want

What Babies Want

Five Simple Steps to Calming and Communicating with Your Baby

Debby Takikawa, DC
and Carrie Contey, PhD

Foreword by Phyllis Klaus, MFT, LCSW

LTM
BOOKS

The information in this book is not intended as a substitute for medical advice. If your baby is crying or distressed and you feel there could be a medical problem, please consult your physician immediately. The CALMS method of communication is not intended to take the place of medical care, but it does continue to be useful to you and your baby during illness. It is a good way to reassure and to keep contact with your baby if he or she needs to go through medical procedures or endure the discomfort of being ill.

LTM Books
352 Seventh Avenue
New York, NY 10001

LTM Books is an imprint of LifeTime Media, Inc.
Visit our website at www.lifetimemedia.com or www.ltmbooks.com

Neither LifeTime Media nor any of its goods or services are in any way affiliated with, associated with, sponsored by or approved by Lifetime networks, Lifetime television, or Lifetime Entertainment series.

ISBN: 9780981636825

Library of Congress Control Number: 2010932931

All LTM Books and LifeTime Media titles are available for special promotions, premiums, and bulk purchase. For more information, please contact the manager of our sales department at 212-631-7524 or sales@lifetimemedia.com

Distributed to the trade by Perseus Book Group
To order books for the trade, call 1-800-343-4499

Printed in the United States of America

10   9   8   7   6   5   4   3   2   1

JUL . . 2012

We dedicate this book to our parents,
partners, and children (present and future),
and the real-life experiences of relationships
we've shared together.

Contents

Foreword....ix

Introduction....xiii

PART ONE   CALMS: Five Simple Steps to Harmony....1

PART TWO   Why Do CALMS?....39

PART THREE   Brain Development, Bonding and Attachment....61

PART FOUR   When Things Don't Go as Planned....79

PART FIVE   Learning to Understand Your Baby....101

PART SIX   Parenting Questions & Answers....127

Acknowledgements....139

References....141

Index....145

Foreword

It is a pleasure to write the foreword for this special book. It is simple but profound, small but filled with important information. In *What Babies Want,* Carrie Contey and Debby Takikawa help parents understand the needs, moods, changes, and rhythms of their infants. Parents learn how to help their baby move from being distressed to a calmer state.

There is wisdom in recognizing your own feelings when entering your child's world. Babies' responses are like a barometer to their parents' or caretakers' emotions. New research has shown that during the whole first year of life there are transfers in emotions and physiological reactions from the right brain of the mother to the right brain of the baby.

All emotional responses have value. All become available from the early development of the limbic system in the womb. Emotions are protective. When an infant is upset, it means that something doesn't feel right at a basic level of survival. Infants cannot put an intellectual meaning to their emotions; they can only feel them throughout their bodies. When overly upset their heart rate goes up, stress hormones increase, and their little systems struggle to handle what may appear to them to be danger.

Unlike us, an infant's system is more fragile. It is immature and doesn't re-regulate quickly. If a baby is stressed too long, he or she may look quiet, but in reality could be having a micro-depression. The immune system can be lowered, and other reactions, such as tummy aches, can occur. It is truly important to recognize "messages" from your baby when he or she is upset. These messages are not verbal nor understood intellectually by the baby; they are felt experiences. The baby needs your help to return to a more stable state. This book provides an easy-to-follow method to do this.

Contey and Takikawa, both knowledgeable caregivers, teach parents how to respond sensitively to their infants, by first being aware of their own feelings, and then by using simple ways to reduce stress, even under trying conditions. The authors show how to acknowledge the baby's experience through gentle mirroring and a variety of other useful methods that will help the baby return to a calmer state.

These thoughtful, helpful methods—checking in with one's self and taking a moment to settle, listening to what the baby is communicating, reflecting back what you are perceiving, then offering comfort—are the basis of good communication. When practiced, they allow parents to work together in mind, body, and emotion to validate a sense of self in the baby. This type of care creates deep and lasting bonds between parents and their children.

PHYLLIS KLAUS, MFT, LCSW

Coauthor:
Your Amazing Newborn
Bonding: Building the Foundations of Secure Attachment and Independence
The Doula Book: How a Trained Labor Companion Can Help You Have a
       Shorter, Easier, and Healthier Birth

Introduction

Around the time of birth, for a few precious moments, we are sometimes able to tap into something so ancient, primal and wise, that we are able
to transcend our limited view of what's possible.

—NOAH WYLE, NARRATION,
WHAT BABIES WANT, THE MOVIE

Welcome and congratulations on the arrival of your new baby.
We are honored to share this book with you and hope it will
provide guidance and inspiration during this tender time of life
and beyond.

It is an exciting time to be a new parent. We know more
about babies and development than ever before. In fact, there
is a revolution taking place in the way we think about and care
for babies. At the core of this transformation is the understanding that your baby is a person who arrived from the womb

with likes and dislikes, feelings and opinions, and an incredible ability to understand and communicate with you. Pause for just a moment and think about the fact that your baby is a whole person. When you keep this in mind, it changes how you are with your baby.

This book is for parents as well as anyone who will be interacting with your baby. It is intended to be an accessible, concrete guide to understanding how to be with your baby in ways that support both of you as you create a deep and loving relationship right from the start.

CALMS is a simple five step approach to support parents and caregivers to calming and communicating with their babies. The five steps of CALMS are:

Check in with yourself.

Allow a breath.

Listen to your baby.

Make contact and mirror feelings.

Soothe your baby.

We have divided this book into six parts. In Part I, we will guide you through the CALMS steps and provide the hows and whys of the method. We will also introduce you to Anna, Mike, and their baby Joshua to illustrate how CALMS can be applied in real life. Part II will offer basic information about human development. In Part III, we focus on early brain development, bonding, and attachment. Part IV addresses the challenges that can happen around birth and guides you in applying the CALMS method for building your relationship with yourself, your baby, and your family. In Part V, we explain how babies communicate and develop language. In this section we provide examples of ways to connect with your little one. Finally, in Part VI, we offer the answers to some common questions about the CALMS method.

Please note that we have alternated the use of "he" and "she" in each section so that it feels personal to all readers.

We have had a wonderful time putting our hearts and heads together to create this book, which honors your baby and your entire family. We respectfully present these ideas to you and hope that our words will be helpful as you find your way into parenthood.

DEBBY AND CARRIE

PART ONE

CALMS:
Five Simple Steps
to Harmony

**Making the decision to have a child is momentous.
It is to decide forever to have a heart go walking
around outside your body.**

—ELIZABETH STONE, AUTHOR

Anna and Mike are the new parents of Joshua, who is now four weeks old. They had a long, hard labor and birth, but there were no serious complications; they came home from the hospital the next day. Joshua is an adorable newborn, with a little crest of black hair, pink cheeks, and sparkling eyes. From his first day at home, Joshua tended to be a bit sensitive about any changes in his routine, and would cry and struggle as he tried to go to sleep. He often woke up crying or fussy. In spite of this, he usually slept a lot and was able to soothe easily with breastfeeding, bouncing, and being carried in the sling. Although they were starting to feel the effects of sleep deprivation, Anna and Mike were having a wonderful time falling in love with this magnificent new baby. Life with Joshua suited them, and after two weeks of being home, Mike was sad about having to return to work.

Since Mike went back to work, Anna has been home alone with Joshua most days. At first, things went smoothly, but as the days go on, Anna has grown more tired and Joshua has grown fussier. The late afternoons have been particularly challenging for both of them. For several days now, Joshua has been crying for over an hour; none of Anna's soothing and calming techniques seem to be working. Trying to handle this alone has not been easy for Anna, and she is wondering if she is doing something wrong, maybe spoiling him with too much attention. She is beginning to lose her confidence as a mother as Joshua gets harder and harder to console.

Today is a particularly challenging day. She anxiously awaits Mike's return from work. She wants him to realize that it isn't so easy to be home alone with the baby all day, and she needs relief from the afternoons of crying. Her shoulders are tight, her throat is constricted, and she is exhausted. This is not what she expected of motherhood.

The minute Mike walks in the door, Anna greets him with, "Oh good. You're home. It's been a hard day, and I really need you to hold Joshua for a little while."

Mike's job is stressful, and he is tired when he gets home. He could use a few minutes to shift from work mode to baby-care mode, but he can tell Anna has been struggling for the last few days, and the stress is starting to get to him too. He feels pressured to dive right in. "Sure, honey, what happened, are you guys all right? How are things going?" He takes Joshua, lays him over his shoulder, and heads to the kitchen to get a drink of water.

At this point everyone is feeling frazzled.

After several afternoons and evenings with a fussy baby, Anna and Mike are feeling overwhelmed. They are both beginning to wonder, *are we doing something wrong? Is there something wrong with our baby? Why didn't anyone tell us it was going to be this challenging?*

Whether your story is similar or quite different from Anna and Mike's, we want you to know that we understand what it is like to struggle with a new baby and feel unsure about what you are doing. Most parents have times when they are unsure about what to do. Part of parenting is wondering what is right for your baby and what will help him grow up to be the best person he can be.

Your Parenting Journey

There are many parenting strategies to choose from; however, no matter which one you pick, it is your relationship with your baby that is most meaningful. Her physical, mental, and emotional well-being are based on the way you connect and interact with her. Our current understanding of infant development very clearly indicates that healthy development depends on consistent, loving, respectful interaction. In writing this book, our intention is to provide you with the support and information you will need to begin connecting and communicating with your baby from birth. Although we are here to provide ideas about how to do that, as parents, you instinctively know your baby and what is right. Trust your feelings and follow your heart; listen to your inner voice. The quieter you get and the more you listen, the more you will know intuitively.

Shifting from Shushing to Listening

"Who is this baby, how can I be connected to this child, and how can I understand what he needs?" When you ask these questions you shift your awareness away from "What do I need to do to this baby to get him to be quiet and content?" toward "I'm in a state of learning about who this person is and what he needs in order to feel safe and secure." If you make the focus of your work as a parent to slow yourself down and tune in to your baby, you will discover that your baby is telling you what he needs.

The CALMS protocol is designed to help you open up to trusting yourself and listening to your baby. Babies are much more sophisticated, sensitive, and communicative than we might think. Knowing how aware they are changes how we interact with them. This book is about how to make that change.

Safety First

Your baby's most basic drive is to survive, and her first need is to know that she is safe. When we think about how to take care of a crying baby, we often go through the checklist of feeding, diapering, and physical comfort. These are important considerations, but secondary to your baby's need for safety. That's why the first step to calming a baby is to let her know that all is well.

The catch to this is, however, that although babies are more sensitive, communicative, and aware than we have given them credit for, they are not operating out of intellect; therefore, this communication about safety must come in a form that the baby understands. Mere words will not convey this to her. Your little infant knows she is safe when she senses that you feel settled and calm.

Babies understand and actually mimic and internalize their parents' inner states by reading their subtle expressions and body language cues. Body language is a powerful means of communication and accurately conveys our inner feelings. If you are feeling stressed or unsettled, your baby is tuning into that. Because safety is the first need, nature has provided us with this survival mechanism: the ability to sense and react to how others are feeling. When you are calm and settled, your baby will know that she is safe, which will help her settle, too. This is why the first two steps of CALMS are focused on you, not your baby. When you start to move toward balance, your baby feels you relax and she will begin to settle. This is the single most important thing you can do to begin the process of soothing your baby.

Acknowledging Your Baby

The next two steps create the kind of communication that affirms your baby's experience. Opening your heart, listening with all of your senses, tuning in to your instincts, and patiently hearing your baby's voice are all part of this process. Listening to your baby in this way acknowledges your baby and helps him to know that you care about what he is experiencing. Now that your baby knows that all is well and that you are willing to hear what he has to say, you will find that he is much more receptive to the fifth step, soothing. Soothing is the next level of need fulfillment, and includes food, comfort, rocking, play, and whatever else you have already discovered that he loves about life.

C
A
L
M
S

STEP 1
Check in with yourself

STEP 2
Allow a breath

STEP 3
Listen to your baby

STEP 4
Make contact and mirror feelings

STEP 5
Soothe your baby

CALMS

STEP 1. Check in with Yourself

When your baby is upset and you are not able to calm her, it can be quite stressful for everyone. Because a baby's cries are meant to evoke a response, it is normal to feel anxious and overwhelmed when you hear them. However, it can be much more difficult to calm your baby if you are not calm yourself. The first step is to check in with yourself, take a pause, and begin to identify your own feelings. Slowing your pace and accepting where you are *right now* is the key to being able to initiate change.

How to Check In

Checking in with yourself is the first step in the process of calming and connecting with your baby.

Ask some basic questions and be honest with yourself. Are you feeling:

Scared	Helpless	Guilty	Sad
Angry	Stuck	Hopeless	Stressed
Frustrated	Inadequate	Distracted	Irritable

If you are feeling any of these feelings, the next step is to pay attention to your body sensations. For example, if you are feeling sad, ask yourself, *where do I feel sadness in my body?* Your body carries information about your feelings that your mind does not normally recognize. Scan your body for tension and other sensations such as tightness, aching, heat, pain, tingling, prickling, or dullness. You might notice these feelings anywhere in your body, but the following areas are a good place to start: jaw, throat, shoulders, hands, stomach, pelvis, and heart/chest.

Most parents experience tense feelings and uncomfortable sensations in these areas at some time or another. It's normal and natural to feel emotionally overwhelmed and physically uncomfortable when you are experiencing stress.

Acknowledging these feelings and finding the areas of tension are two ways to begin letting go of your stress. Just take it one step at a time.

Why Check In?

Your feelings form a bridge between you and your baby. Because your baby's cries can activate your own stress response, it is important to notice your stress and begin to understand it. Honestly acknowledging your feelings and sensations is a first step toward feeling calmer. Your baby will feel this shift because on an emotional level he is exquisitely tuned in to you. As you take this first step toward calming and settling yourself, your baby will notice the change and begin to settle with you. Taking this time allows you to establish mutual feelings of peace and love.

Checking In

Let's return to Anna, Mike, and Joshua, the family we met in the beginning of this section.

When we left off, Anna, Mike, and Joshua were having a really tough time. Sensing that they needed to do something to shift the mood, they start the CALMS steps. The first thing Mike does is check in with himself; he realizes that he is exhausted, frustrated, and feeling ineffective. He notices his shoulders are hunched and his lower back is tight. It crosses his mind that he's lost his touch, and he wonders, *does Joshua only want to be with Anna?*

Meanwhile, Anna has started cooking dinner. She thought she was going to be relieved to pass Joshua on to Mike, but as she checks in with herself, she realizes that it's the sound of his crying that is evoking her feelings of anxiety. She's afraid to admit that she's worried that she's not a good mother, and wonders if she will be able to give Joshua what he needs. Her throat feels tight, her stomach is in knots, and she's on the verge of tears. Her inclination is to keep going and work on dinner but something inside of her says, "Just sit with the feelings for a minute."

CALMS

STEP 2. Allow a Breath

Once you have checked in with yourself, take several deep breaths and allow things to simply be just as they are in this moment. Don't try to force a change. Trust that the change is coming. In the act of performing these simple steps, you are practicing "self-care" and intentionally calming yourself down. Slowing your body and mind and soothing yourself is a process. Different methods work for different people. We recommend trying some of the suggestions offered below and using what works for you.

How to Allow a Breath

You can allow yourself a breath with your eyes open or closed, sitting or standing, and just about anywhere:

- Deeply inhale for a four-count, and then exhale for as long as you can.
- Imagine that a sense of calm is entering and flowing through your body with each intake of breath.
- Do this three to five times, and repeat as needed.

C
A
L
M
S

Here are a few more ways you can practice self-care:

- Slowly drink a glass of water.

- Look out the window.

- Go outside for some air.

- Eat a healthy snack.

- Feel your feet on the floor.

- Tighten and relax your fists.

- Make eye contact with another adult.

- Get a hug or some physical contact from another adult.

- Call a supportive, empathetic friend or family member.

- Use positive self-talk: "I can do this." "My baby wants my help." "I am doing my best."

Sometimes getting to that calm place takes a few moments and many deep breaths. It may be necessary to turn your attention inward and away from your baby while you do these first two steps. As long as your baby is safe in your arms or on the bed, it is all right to take a few moments to care for yourself. This turning inward is an essential part of the process of calming your baby. She is feeling and reacting to your emotional states. When you feel tense, she feels anxious. When you feel settled, she feels safe. When you allow a breath and calm yourself down, she begins to breathe more easily as well. As she begins to settle, her body feels better, her stomach relaxes, and she receives better circulation for better digestion.

Additional Exercises

Here are two more ways that you can practice slowing down and coming back to yourself:

- Focus on your heart and make space in your chest by inhaling again. Visualize the last time your baby was calm and asleep on your chest. Imagine the sensation of her warm little head on your chest and how good you felt, and take another deep breath.

C
A
L
M
S

- Imagine that your emotions and physical state are connected to an internal volume knob that you can slowly and gently turn down. When you are doing things to soothe your baby who seems to have a hard time settling, you can try turning down your "emotional volume."

Why Allow a Breath?

In the early stage of your baby's life, he is developing the ability to regulate his emotions. He is doing this in relationship with you. He is not equipped to settle alone. At this point, he needs and benefits from your help. Your baby is still forming and learning how to manage all of his emotional ups and downs. Because he is tuning in to you and your feelings, each time you go through an upsetting time with him, you have an opportunity to help your baby organize his emotions. When you stay connected with your little one and start to settle your own body, your baby will copy you. Taking a few moments for deep breathing and self-care during such times can be just what you both need to get back to a place of balance. When you are feeling balanced, you can be more effective in helping your baby settle, and feel safe and comfortable again.

Allowing a Breath

While holding Joshua in his arms, Mike allows a breath, and another, and another. He slips his shoes off and feels his feet on the floor. With each breath, his system settles just a bit. He also checks in with his body. He notices that his heart is racing and his shoulders are very tight. He specifically tries to focus his breathing into those areas. Mike reminds himself that right now he is feeling stressed and being with Joshua is a challenge. He also tells himself that he is a good dad and can take care of a crying baby. He continues breathing. This is not easy because Joshua is still crying, but he sticks with it.

Anna is appreciating herself for also taking a little pause and realizes that as she begins to breathe with her feelings, they dissipate. Her breathing deepens. She looks over to her husband and son and feels her deep appreciation for Mike and Joshua.

CALMS

STEP 3. Listen to Your Baby

Now that you have checked in with yourself and practiced a few moments of self-care, it's time to listen to your baby and to ask the question, "What are you trying to tell me, little one?" Your baby is a whole person with feelings and emotions; she is speaking a language that may in some ways be foreign to you. Her main way to communicate is through body language, facial expressions, sounds, and crying. You are learning her language, and although you may not immediately know what she is trying to say, it is very important to her that you are trying to understand what she is communicating. It might take some practice to feel proficient at deciphering her language, but trust that you will get there. You are one of the main people in her life, and she wants you to know what is happening and how she is feeling.

We know how challenging it can be to hear your baby crying and not understand what she needs, but by listening to your baby, you will be able to learn something about what she needs. This may be a new idea, a new way of thinking about parenting. It can be mystifying to communicate with this little person who does not speak your language. You are going to have to rely on your senses, observations, feelings, and intuitions.

Please note that the following listening and mirroring steps go hand-in-hand. You may find it useful to alternate back and forth between these two steps as the conversation develops between you and your baby.

How to Listen

Here are some simple tips for beginning the process of listening to your baby:

- Slow down.
- Become quiet inside.
- Use all of your senses to observe your baby.
- Pay attention to what your inner voice is telling you.
- Trust your instinct.

The first step to listening to your baby is to become quiet inside. Be patient, especially with yourself. Observe your baby's pacing, breathing, and body tension. Look at your baby and see the details of facial expression, body movement. Hear the sounds of the cry. Be willing to learn about your baby, and for the moment put aside the need to stop your baby's crying. Right now your job is to stay with yourself and to listen and watch your baby very carefully with an open mind. Give your baby time to express himself, and give yourself time to really take it all in.

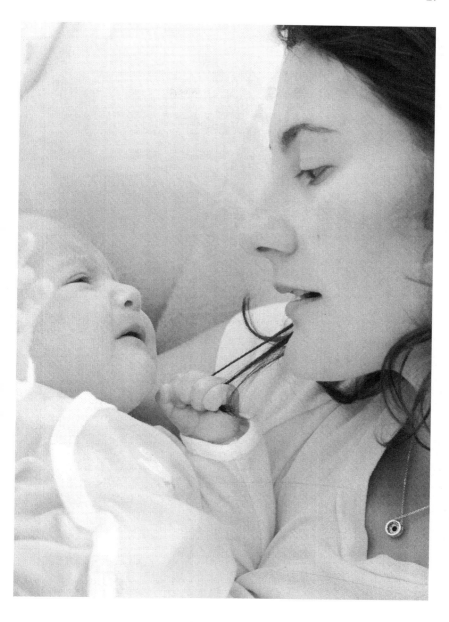

Why Listen?

When you begin to understand what your baby is telling you, you can better meet her needs. Even if you don't understand her right away, your baby will be reassured to know that you are listening. When a small baby has genuinely responsive parents who see her as a person, it gives her a feeling of recognition and self-worth. The result is that she feels safe and loved.

New research has provided us with information about the complexities and awareness of babies, and how actively they are reaching out to connect with their parents. Even though they arrive in tiny, vulnerable bodies, we can interact with them. Although you and your baby are not speaking the same language, remember that your baby is trying to communicate her feelings and needs to you. She is intelligent and will try many ways to get you to understand her. The best you can give her is your respect and sincere effort to listen. As you sincerely listen and respond, you may find yourself in a new world of communication with your baby that can be quite remarkable and exciting.

Listening

As Mike's body starts to settle, and he turns his focus toward Joshua, he recognizes how vulnerable and frantic Joshua is feeling. Once he makes that shift from feeling inadequate into realizing that Joshua is having a tough time, he feels curious about what is happening for him.

"What's going on with you little man? How can I help you?" he says.

Joshua continues to cry but seems less frantic. Mike starts to realize that he is not causing Joshua's upset feelings, and this allows him to be more present. He thinks to himself, *Wow, this little dude is really trying to tell me something.*

Anna has started cooking dinner and realizes that Joshua's cry has taken on a different tone. He seems less upset. She can hear Mike talking to him and looks over to see what they're doing. Mike notices Anna and says, "Seems like he just wanted me to slow down and start listening."

CALMS

STEP 4. Make Contact and Mirror Feelings

Now that you have reached this step, you are ready to interact with your baby in a way that you may never have considered doing before. Even though you have been talking to your baby, probably since before birth, now you are going to respond to your baby's cues. The variety of ideas presented here are only suggestions and possible scenarios. Listening and responding to your baby from your heart is what really works.

How to Make Contact and Mirror Feelings

Here are some simple ways to begin the process of making contact and mirroring what your baby is showing you:

- Think about what you hear, see, and feel as you observe and listen to your baby.
- Make comforting physical contact with your baby.
- Talk to your baby about what you think is going on.

- Leave your communication open-ended: "It seems like you feel . . ." or "It looks like . . ." or "I wonder if . . ."

- Keep the dialogue going by checking in again and noticing your baby's response to your words.

- Notice your own feelings and keep breathing.

- Continue cycling through the listening and mirroring steps for as long as it feels productive.

For example, you might notice that your baby is really scrunching up his face and holding his fists tight. You might say, "I see how scrunched up your face is and how tight you are holding your fists." When you have said that, it is useful to come back to the listening step. Your baby will respond to what you have just said. If you listen again, you will see what your baby does in response to being heard and reflected by you. It's a simple conversation, but it can lead to a lifetime of sharing! As you carry on this conversation with your baby, he will calm and settle, or if he has a complaint, he will be more able to maintain contact while he tells you about it. Most people know that you can talk to a baby, but what they don't realize is that the baby will answer.

Here are some examples of mirroring phrases that might be reflective. Keep in mind your baby will respond best when you reflect the movements you see and feelings you feel while listening to him. Your simple and genuine communication—the words you say and the way you say them, the expressions on your face and the way you move your body—conveys all of the information that your baby needs in order to understand your reflection:

- "Oh, baby, you are having a tough time."
- "I really hear you."
- "Yes, baby, you are really upset. I see how upset you are."
- "I see that your eyes are closed and your face is scrunched."
- "I see how you are kicking your legs and moving your arms by your head."
- "You seem really frustrated right now."
- "That was a loud noise, and it startled you."
- "I can see and hear that you are really crying."
- "I see you looking at me."
- "Wow, that's a big smile."
- "Oh, looking away."
- "That was a deep breath."
- "Big stretch!"

You've been listening. You may not quite know what you are listening for or understand what your baby is saying; however, you don't need all the answers to begin to mirror your child's expression. Just a simple reflection of "Oh, I see your eyes are closed" might be enough to get the conversation going. The great thing about mirroring is that initially you don't have to know the meaning of the expression or movement. Just describe what you see. It's a tool for starting the conversation. You may not get all the information on the first try, but by getting even part of the message and mirroring it back, your baby will often have a distinct response of connection, excitement, or relief. As you let your baby know what you have seen and heard from him, keep on listening and watching for his response to what you are saying now. The communication builds by going back and forth between listening and mirroring or responding.

Let your baby know you hear him and see how he is feeling. Be genuine and believe that your baby is trying to communicate. This step is about validating his experience and empathizing with him.

Although your baby might continue to cry as you are talking, you may notice that he is making more eye contact, or that the sound of the cry is changing. Reflect this as well. In the case of eye contact, you might say in a pleasant but not overly playful voice, "Oh look, I see you looking at me," or "Hi there, little one," or "Thanks for looking at me." This kind of response keeps your baby in contact with you. Now that he knows you are watching him, he will try to give you more information.

Another thing that your baby might do is try to push away or hide his face. Respond to his body language. If you are trying to breast-feed and he is pushing away, you might tell him that even though you think he is hungry, you do not want to make him eat if he is not ready. Let him know that you are

willing to wait, and that you have time to find out what he needs. Take your lead from his body language and the situation. As you practice doing this with your baby, you will be amazed to find out that you can carry on quite a complex conversation. Just keep on listening and reflecting back.

Why Make Contact and Mirror Feelings?

Your baby is flooded with new experiences, sensations, and emotions. Digestive pain, loud surroundings, growing bones, emerging teeth, and confusing emotions swirling around from the people nearby are all affecting her. She is looking for herself amidst the commotion, and she is working to find a way to integrate this newness. The main way babies learn to see themselves is through the eyes of others. When you connect to your baby and reflect to her what you see happening, it can be orienting for her. With your help, she can find her own center and grow from the inside out.

We all know how wonderful it feels when the person who is caring for us is tuned in and trying to match our feelings. Most people have a deep longing to be seen, heard, and responded to in this kind and gentle way. It is validating and helps us open ourselves to love. This type of respect is important for a positive sense of self. Your baby's sense of self and ability to love grows from feelings of connection and validation.

Making Contact and Mirroring

Now that Mike has slowed himself down and is able to look at Joshua's experience as something he can interact with, he tries mirroring. He says, "Joshua, sweet boy, I hear that you are upset. I've been feeling anxious and stressed, too." Mike pauses, breathes, and thinks back to his earlier impression of Joshua. He says, "It sounds like you might be feeling pretty overwhelmed." As Joshua looks up and wails at his dad, Mike says, "Yeah, that's hard." Joshua buries his face in his father's chest. Mike pauses for a moment, takes a breath, and says, "I see how you are burrowing your face into my chest. You are safe, and I'm here to protect and take care of you, little guy. Nothing else really matters right now."

As Mike says this, he realizes that his worries at work are less important, and he finds himself totally in the moment with his baby boy. Joshua looks up at Mike, and his crying slows down. He is listening to his father's voice and feeling the settling that his father is experiencing. He is not done crying, but the sounds of his cries are changing. He is starting to pay more attention to Mike and his eyes are open now.

Feeling relieved, relaxed, and hopeful, Anna walks over to join her guys. She says to Joshua, "You seem like you are calming down with your daddy." She turns to Mike, gives him tender kiss and says, "Thank you."

CALMS

STEP 5. Soothe
Your Baby

Now that you are calmer and connecting with your baby, it is likely that he will be more able to receive and benefit from the comforting measures you have to offer. Usually at this point your baby wants to find a way to stop crying. He has been heard and responded to, and he will be more able to integrate the help he needs to calm down and settle in. He may still need to cycle through the crying again, but now he is doing it with support from you, and you no longer feel like a frustrated, helpless bystander.

If your baby is still crying, continue to follow the first four steps of CALMS—check in with yourself, allow more breaths, listen to your baby, and continue to mirror what he is showing you. Don't despair: crying is one possible normal response to soothing and actually can be very healing. Please trust yourself and your baby, and know that your interactions are meaningful and have a positive effect. Let your infant know that you hear him and understand how upset he is. Know that you have done good work by listening, supporting, and connecting with your baby. You will find that once he has released his feelings and been heard by you, he may be ready for the soothing you offer and most likely a deep, relaxing sleep. And don't forget that you have been through a lot too, and it is time for some self-care.

How to Soothe

As your child's parent you already have effective tricks and tools for soothing your baby. Here are some simple reminders of the basics:

- Holding
- Breast-feeding or close body contact
- Sweet sounds such as poems or songs
- Being worn in a sling
- Bouncing
- Rocking
- Going outside, feeling fresh air, and seeing plants and animals
- Hearing white noise such as running water or radio static

Here are some ideas for how to make your soothing efforts more effective:

- Let your baby know that you are going to try one of the things that usually helps to calm and soothe her.

- Watch her response and notice if she starts the calming and settling.

- Be sure that you are offering, not pushing, the soothing activity onto your baby.

- Continue to listen and reflect as you enter into the soothing activity.

- Give each activity some time for your baby to adapt to it.

It is important to continue your conversation with your baby as you offer soothing behaviors. Let your baby know what you are going to do before you do it, and be sure to continue to observe how your baby is responding. For example, if you offer the breast and your baby is pushing up with her feet, mirror this back to your baby. You might say, "Oh I see you wanting to push," and put your hands on your baby's feet so that she can push against you. She might need some physical movement before she can settle in to feed. Once you begin to notice your baby's cues, you will be more likely to appropriately respond to her communications and meet her needs. It is so important to trust your baby and your own parenting instincts.

Why Soothe?

Although your baby needs to be heard and acknowledged, he also needs to be soothed. All babies are born with very immature nervous systems. During his first several years, your baby relies on you to be his external regulatory system; in other words, he is expecting and needing you to activate his calming responses. Eventually he will learn to do this for himself, but in the beginning he needs help. That is why you feel so compelled to help your baby when he is crying. It's instinctive.

Even though you want to fix everything for your baby, it is not always possible. Sometimes he will simply need to experience his feelings. Being held, cared for, listened to, and acknowledged by a calm, loving person in the midst of intense feelings brings your baby's system back into balance. What you can do is be there and let your baby know that you are trying your best to stay present and connected, and to understand him. When his needs are met, it sends his brain the message that he is in a world that is friendly and responsive.

Conclusion

Each time that you go through the process of CALMS, you and your baby will learn more about each other. As a result, you will be more able to soothe and help her through those hard times. As your baby learns that you are there for her when she is struggling, her trust will deepen knowing you will be there for her in every mood and at every turn. This is trust learned at a very deep, essential level in your child's psyche. Because your child is still in a very formative period, the trust learned during this early time is incorporated into her development and becomes a way of being for her. Her experience of your calmness and presence will enhance her ability to be calm and present with herself. With practice, she will become more at ease with your routines and daily activities of her life. This kind of attention will offer your child an emotional foundation of safety and security, and a belief that she lives in a world she can trust.

CALMS IN ACTION

Soothing

As everyone continues to calm down, Mike notices that Joshua is rooting around on his chest. Anna realizes that it's been about two hours since he has eaten and suggests that she sit down before dinner and offer him some milk. Mike kisses Joshua, hands him to Anna, and tells her that he'll finish cooking dinner. A few minutes later Mike puts dinner on the table, and Joshua is sound asleep in Anna's arms.

PART TWO

Why Do CALMS?

The second he came out when he heard Tracy's voice, he picked his head up and looked in her direction and then when I spoke he turned his head and looked in my direction.

—NOAH WYLE, ACTOR NARRATION
WHAT BABIES WANT, THE MOVIE

In order to fully understand how CALMS works, it is important to understand this new view of how we unfold as human beings. This perspective comes not only from our own work with families, but from the work of many therapists, researchers, neuroscientists, and teachers past and present. Understanding that babies come into the world as conscious, awake, and aware beings helps us to be kind, gentle, and patient with our young ones.

For a long time our culture has viewed babies in a limited way. Babies were seen as:

- Passive passengers in the womb and for some time after birth.

- Not possessing enough brain structure to express meaningful communication and learn or maintain memories before they are able to speak.

- Unable to experience pain.

- Arriving as a "blank slate."

Children clearly recognize that there is someone inside.

Now, however, new and exciting knowledge about infants is emerging. Discoveries made in the twentieth century in fields such as prenatal psychology, embryology, neurobiology, and attachment theory have changed our world view about babies and human development. We are gaining a much deeper understanding of who babies really are and what they are capable of doing, feeling, knowing, and experiencing.

Our current understanding of babies, based on this new perspective, includes the following assumptions:

- Babies are sensitive and aware in the womb and beyond.

- The newborn arrives as a whole person on a lifelong continuum of development.

- Memory is being created through the emotions and the senses from the very beginning.

- Experiences before, during, and after birth have a direct effect on lifelong physical and psychological health.

- A baby's earliest experiences and interactions with parents and caregivers influence how the brain and nervous system develop.

This new recognition of a baby's abilities and sensitivities is teaching us to pay much closer attention to what our babies are thinking and feeling. The indications are that babies are much more cognizant, at a much earlier age, than we ever imagined. What we are learning now is that babies are responding, learning, and communicating right from the beginning, and interactive

Basic essence.

experiences actually stimulate healthy development, especially brain development. This rich expression does not happen in isolation; rather, it is happening in their relationships with parents and caregivers. These exchanges of communication are the foundational building blocks of emotional, physical, and mental well-being. This new understanding offers us an evolutionary way of thinking about and being with babies.

Babies Are People

Your baby is a person. His basic essence is always there, from the beginning of life until the end. Development is the unfolding of his ability to express what is already present and active in him from the beginning. When you look at your newborn baby, you may be taken with how vulnerable he seems. His physical abilities are so limited that it might be easy to overlook the big being in the little body. During these early days, you might be more aware of the ways he is different from you, but there are also many ways that he is the same. For example, he is unable to speak, but he finds ways of communicating. He cannot feed himself, but he shows you when he is hungry. He cannot move from place to place without your assistance right now, but soon he will be moving around on his own.

Your baby's brain and body are working as fast as they can to develop in order to give him the freedom to express himself in ways you will be able to understand, and to express who he really is and what he is here to do in this world. Within weeks after birth he will be laughing and smiling. Within months he will be moving around on his own. Within a year he will be eating most of the foods that you eat, and within two years he will be running around and working toward speaking in sentences. If you watch your baby, you will see that even now he is working really hard to master all of these skills.

Once you realize that your baby is a whole person, it changes the way you interact with him and enhances his ability to be himself in the world. You include him in the conversations. You attribute more importance to his needs. You think about how your actions are affecting him, and you respect him more fully.

Nature and Nurture

The question of nature versus nurture has long been debated in an effort to understand how humans develop. What determines who we will become: our essential nature and our genes, or our environment? Currently many researchers agree that human development is an ongoing interplay between nature and nurture. Our essential nature and our genetics provide us with a core of being. This is the nature part of life. As we grow, we develop a network of nerves that connect our brain structure, and our body systems mature under the influence of environmental pressure. This is the nurture part of life.

The core of being is potent and alive with possibility. It is our deepest part, and it forms what we identify as self. Your baby comes into the world already trying to express herself in every way that she can. At birth she is limited by physical ability, which must be somewhat frustrating. Even so, right from the beginning, your baby is expressing herself and letting you know who she is. Her character, preferences, and general approach to life are all visible if you know what to look for. Most parents will say that when they look into the eyes of their new baby they can see that this baby is her own person, different from all others they have known. This might be describing the nature aspect of a person.

The effect of the environment and the care your baby receives is the nurture aspect of life. This part of her development helps her formulate her ability to express her inner nature. The nurture aspect includes the influence of the environment and relationships. The way you nurture your baby profoundly influences how she uses her body and mind to connect with the world and to be a part of your family and the human family. This begins during gestation when a baby's experiences are filtered through her mother. At birth she begins to experience the environment more directly but continues to rely on her mother for cues about the environment. She also connects with and deepens relationships with the people close to her.

Nature is our core, and nurture powerfully influences how that core is expressed. We believe that healthy development is the interplay of both nature and nurture.

Babies Are Sensing

Your baby arrived from the womb an extraordinarily sensitive being. He uses all of his senses (sight, smell, sound, taste, and touch) to learn about his environment. During the early months before he can speak, this sensing is the way he gathers information about the world in which he lives.

For most babies, the world is a very busy, bright, and noisy place. Over time we, as adults, have learned to tune out a lot of what is going on around us. Because your baby is so sensitive and open to learning, he cannot do that yet. As a result, if the environment is overly stimulating, for example, the lights are too bright or there is too much noise, your baby may become overwhelmed. When this happens, he will often let you know by crying or just shutting down and going to sleep until things are more at a level he can manage. Tuning in to your baby's unique tolerance for sensory stimulation is very important to his well-being. Bringing him slowly and willingly into the outside world will help his nervous system to integrate what he is experiencing.

Babies Learn How to Make Sense of Their Feelings From the People Who Care For Them

Because your baby cannot yet assess the outside world very well, she will tune in to the one thing she knows—you. Your baby will sense if things are safe or unsafe, happy or sad, or fun or dangerous by tuning in to your emotional state and responding based on your reactions.

To illustrate this point, imagine walking into a room and seeing someone you love. You can often sense how that person is feeling. This sensing is commonly referred to as a "gut feeling" or intuition; it is a way of knowing, a way of tuning in, and

Sharing a joyful moment.

resonating to the emotional state of another person. All humans are capable of this. Your baby is extra sensitive to how others are feeling because her sense of their feelings lets her know if she is physically and emotionally safe in any given situation.

Because of this sensing by your baby, the first step in the CALMS protocol is checking in with yourself. If you are upset, stressed, hopeless, sad, or angry, your baby will be able to sense this and be affected by those feelings. If, at this stage, you spend a few moments relaxing your body and mind, your baby will soon learn this routine. This is especially important when you are responding to your baby when she is upset. If you approach her with anxiety or alarm, she will sense your reaction and express even more distress. However, if you check in and take a moment to settle yourself she will sense that and will take your cue that all is well, she is safe, and she can calm down.

By repeating this action you have the chance to give your baby the gift early in life of learning how to calm and settle during stressful times. The behaviors your baby learns at this stage will become second nature to her throughout her life. You certainly can't avoid all stress or difficult feelings, but you can help your baby learn how to manage them effectively right from the start by being mindful of how you are feeling when you are caring for your baby.

Sorting Out Feelings

It can be a little disconcerting to think that your baby is so tuned in to you. This does not mean that you always have to be perfect and on guard: your baby can also tell when you are trying to mask your feelings. It's more helpful to be honest and open about your feelings.

When you check in with yourself, you can name and own your feelings. Let your baby know in a simple way what is happening. By taking this step your baby will be free from having to worry about things that are not appropriate for him. You might say something like, "I am upset because I bounced a check, but that doesn't have anything to do with you and I can handle it. I am not upset with you, and we are safe." Even though your baby doesn't understand bouncing checks, your explanation will carry a shift in energy as you own your stress.

The added bonus of naming your situation out loud for your baby is that it can give you a sense of perspective about the problem as well. One of the great things we can learn from being with a baby is to be in this moment, right here, right now. When we take our cues from the baby, we begin to let go of stress and just attend to what is happening in the present. You can still deal with that bounced check—and even be upset or annoyed by it—but the key is to not let that interfere with your emotional interactions with your baby.

Babies Experience Birth

Now that we know how sensitive and aware babies are, birth from the baby's perspective takes on a new meaning. During birth, babies go through an intense transition. No matter how

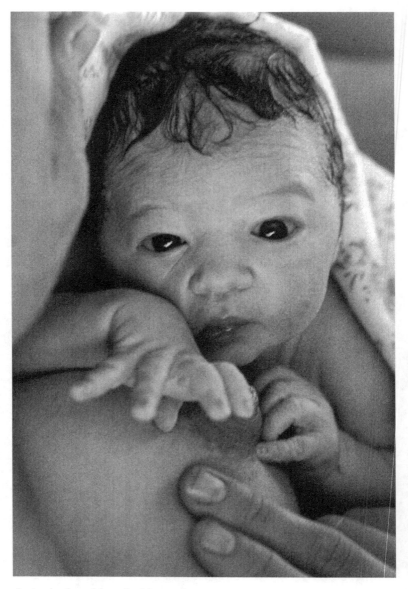

Just minutes old, and wide awake.

your baby is born, the journey to the outside world is profound, resulting in numerous internal and external changes. For example, at birth, every one of your baby's senses, especially her skin, is exposed to new and heightened stimuli. Your baby immediately begins to breathe on her own, using her lungs for the first time, which changes the way her heart circulates blood. When we hold her with the knowledge that she is aware and making an enormous transition, it helps her feel safe.

The way your baby is cared for and welcomed at birth can have a big influence on how she adjusts to the outside environment. Your baby is born with instincts and reflexes that are intended to help her survive—the strongest of which is the desire and will to connect with her mother. At birth she knows to look for her mother's face and is able to recognize her mother's voice, touch, and scent. Just like any other baby mammal, your baby is born with reflexes that will help her connect her to her mother. She has crawling reflexes that will help her move to the breast, and she has rooting and sucking reflexes to help her find the breast and latch on. When she is placed on her mother at birth, she has the experience of having her instinctual needs fulfilled. This, in turn, helps her feel safe and secure.

What Do Babies Want?

Imagine what it would be like to be sensitive and aware of what is happening around you and at the same time physically helpless—unable to get to what you need, go where you want, or tell people how you are feeling. How would you want to be cared for? How would you like the people around you to communicate with you? How would you want to be treated?

Putting yourself in this position will give you a window into the experience your baby is having. He is a person with thoughts, feelings, and needs, yet he cannot express himself in ways that others can easily understand. This is such a vulnerable time of life for your child. What he wants most during this time is to feel safe, loved, and respected as a human being. When people are respectful toward us we feel seen, heard, and valued. Just like us, this is what babies want.

Let's look at some of the ways you are giving your baby what he wants. Physical touch is the best way to communicate safety and love to a brand-new person. When you hold, snuggle, and massage your little one regularly during the day, you are letting him know that you are there and will keep him out of harm's way. Sustained skin-to-skin contact helps build his brain and strengthen all of his vital body systems. Your physical presence is a great way to reassure your baby that all is well. Another way is to verbally communicate directly with your baby. When you verbally reflect what you sense your baby is feeling, you are connecting. Telling your baby what you will be doing with him throughout the course of the day helps your baby feel safe and cared for. When you include your baby in the conversations you are having, especially if you are speaking about him, you are showing him respect.

Gentle loving touch.

Your Baby's Developing Mind

Your baby senses both your physical and emotional presence. In order to fully understand this we need to look at early brain development. By the end of the first trimester, your baby has developed all of the parts of her brain; the next step is to connect all of these parts together. This miraculous connection process occurs throughout life but is most significant during the last few months of gestation and the first three years of childhood. This connecting process does not happen on its own; rather, it is directly linked to our relationships and interactions with our caregivers. As the brain connects through interaction with other humans, it begins to create meaning. With meaning, your baby begins to form a neurological map of her unique world.

In order for your baby to be able to form a strong connection to you, which in turn will influence the healthy development of her brain, it is vital that you learn to perceive and respond to your child's experience and emotional state. In the film *What Babies Want*, well-known author and teacher, Joseph Chilton Pearce says, "You don't have to teach the child emotional intelligence; you have to be it around them. You can't keep the brain from absorbing it." This is why, in the case of stressful experiences, it is useful for the caregiver to be able to take a calming moment. Your baby responds to stress, and if you can calm down, your baby will copy your behavior and incorporate it, actually hardwiring it into her neural structures. It may take many times of consistently doing this,

Tender kisses help soothe emotions.

but your baby will learn and benefit. You are teaching your baby how to work through stressful situations.

What You Can Do With Feelings of Frustration

It is three o'clock in the morning, and your baby has woken up crying every hour for the past three hours. You are jarred out of sleep, feeling exhausted, and unable to cope. As a new parent, there may be times when you feel frustrated, angry, or helpless. It can be very challenging when your baby is crying inconsolably, not sleeping well, having trouble breast-feeding, or just simply growing. Remember, your baby is new at this, too. It is important to let your baby know that your feelings of frustration are about the circumstances of the situation and not about him.

Just as important as it is to support your baby, you need support, too. If you are sleep-deprived and struggling, reach out to trusted friends and relations. It is fine for us to suggest that you just take a breath and relax, but you might need a friend to lean on in order to be able to get your breath! As a new parent you deserve support and help, and should not be expected (or expect yourself) to do everything alone. First, try to lower your expectations of what you think you should get done each day, and nap with your baby. Then, take care of yourself—call a friend, find an online chat group, or connect with a parenting resource center in your town. It helps to talk about your frustrations and challenges, and to know that others are struggling with similar issues.

Crying with contact.

Community Support

Humans are social creatures. These days, with families scattered across the globe, it is important to establish a group of friends and spend time with them. Parents of young children especially benefit from being with other parents. It is very helpful to know that you are not the only one who is sleep-deprived, confused, or frustrated with the challenges of early parenthood. Often other moms and dads have helpful tips and coping skills that can be useful.

It is also important to build relationships with people who understand and are going through similar experiences. Having that level of support on a regular basis is not only very affirming, but actually helps settle and release tension and anxiety, which will help your baby remain calm and settled as well.

When the greater community welcomes your baby and family, it creates a sense of love and security for everyone. Society needs children as much as children need society. Our children represent the future. Being part of a multigenerational community who acknowledge children can make a huge difference for the health of the community. Babies and children want to be in a world where they are welcomed, can express themselves, and be recognized and honored for who they are. Trust your child, believe that her communications are valid, and respond to her in the way that you would like to be responded to. Each human comes into this world with a purpose, a reason for being here. When we see our children this way, they are supported to fulfill their purpose for being here. Recognition and respect from family and community gives them the precious gift of self-worth.

*Community elders welcome and admire
a new baby at the farmers market.*

PART THREE

Brain Development, Bonding, and Attachment

There is a great energy and power and wisdom that comes with the child into the world and awakens the mother in order to awaken the child.

—JOSEPH CHILTON PEARCE, INTERVIEW, *WHAT BABIES WANT,* THE MOVIE

Between conception and age three, your baby will go from a one-celled organism, created out of a microscopically small sperm and egg, into someone who can use all of his senses, create meaningful communication, eat and digest a multitude of foods, regulate body functions, roll over, crawl, sit up, stand up, walk, run, talk, create art and music, sing, express empathy, tell jokes, and so much more! In such a remarkably short time, your child will learn things that will allow him to fully connect with you, express his essential self, and experience life in such a rich and exciting way. In order to understand how this is all possible, let's turn our attention toward what is happening in early brain development.

At conception, a miraculous process begins: the development of your child's physical body. As sperm and egg meet, they fuse together to form a single cell. Within that single cell is the genetic material that will drive the formation of your child's physical development. Three weeks after conception the first brain cells appear. There are two key aspects of this development: the formation of brain structures, and the proliferation and organization of nerve cells. The brain structures include all of the various parts within the brain, each performing a different function. During the early years of life these structures will become a part of the complex web of nerve cells that grow and connect as your baby learns about the world. During gestation, nerve cells are developing at an astounding rate. Your baby will be born with approximately 200 billion nerve cells—the most he will ever have. Underused cells are pruned away so that by adulthood we are left with an average of 100 billion brain cells.

Although some nerve cells are programmed to perform specific functions such as controlling heart beats, breathing, digestion, sight, and taste, the majority are not specialized. It is the environment and not the genes that shape how these unspecialized nerve cells are connected and used.

The experience of birth, and all of the hormonal and sensory changes that accompany this monumental transition, initiates a new phase of brain development. Starting at birth and for the next three years, the billions of nerve cells will develop branches that link together to form a vast network that connects the various structures of the brain. These connections become useful pathways that help your baby to assimilate his experiences.

How does this happen? Sensory experiences ignite the electrical activity that enables the brain to develop connections and grow. Repeated experiences cause the connections to become well-worn pathways permanently etched into the brain. This allows your baby to take in sensory information and to develop his brain so that it is specialized for the environment he lives in. Any road, trail, or pathway is more established the more it is traveled. The same is true for nerve cell connections. The more they are used, the more they become dedicated to that pathway. If the connection is not used, it slowly disappears.

Bonding and Attachment

In this section on bonding and attachment, we would like to offer some basic information on how early care of your baby affects her development. The love, nurturing, and respect you give to your baby supports her brain and nervous system to form into functional tools that she can use for the creative expression of her whole self.

Eye contact stimulates brain development.

It should be acknowledged that for many families living in today's society, birth is challenging. One-third of women in the United States have babies by cesarean section. In addition, many other interventions and circumstances can happen that do not allow for immediate access to your new baby. Many births are not peaceful and calming, even though this may have been the goal of the expectant parents and emerging infant.

Our discussion of bonding depicts a birth in which the mother is awake, oriented, and able to connect to her baby, and where the birth attendants (midwives, doctors, nurses, doulas, and family members) are gentle, conscious, and respectful of the moments of early mother-infant connection. In reality this is rare. It may take hours, days, weeks, or even in some cases, months, for the mother and infant to achieve the calm and profound interactions that we are describing as bonding and attachment. The next chapter touches on some of these challenges.

When you look into your baby's sweet face and are flooded with feelings of love, joy, and appreciation, your baby feels your emotions. During these moments you are in the process of bonding with her. As your baby feels your love and care repeatedly, she begins to settle into the fact that you are there for her to meet her needs. Through these exchanges she begins to develop a secure attachment. These exchanges of love are the building blocks of the long-term process of healthy development.

When you are met with the reality of a baby who cries often or has trouble breast-feeding or digesting food, the heart-based

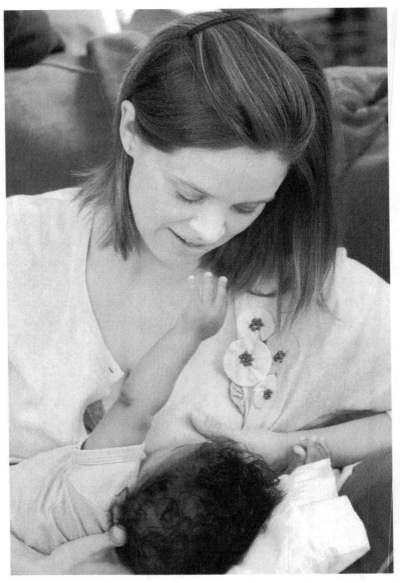

Breast feeding can be a powerful path to connection.

experiences of love, joy, and appreciation you have felt may be overshadowed by feelings of frustration and anxiety. The intention of the CALMS method is simply to help you find your way back to the peaceful place of the heart connection, even in the midst of the challenging times.

Connecting With You:
The Essential Task of the First Year

The foundation of your baby's emotional development is based on the bond that you create with him, which consists of a flow of emotional communication between the two of you. It starts at conception and continues to strengthen as your baby grows and develops. Attachment is the relationship that your baby forms with you and is dependent on the quality of the bonding relationship that you are creating with him. The development of bonding and attachment is the primary undertaking of the first year of your baby's life outside the womb.

Bonding at Birth and Beyond

There are a few peak experiences in a person's life, and one of them is birth. What a triumph for a child to be conceived, develop, and emerge as a whole human ready to experience life.

From the moment your baby is born, you have the opportunity to meet and interact with her. Ideally, this time period

The essential human need for skin-to-skin contact.

allows you and your baby to take a few deep breaths and settle after such an arduous journey. Within minutes after birth your baby will begin to open her awareness to her new surroundings. If you can slow down and tune in to these moments and quietly talk to your baby, you will see her begin to move around and look for you. You can then follow her cues for what kind of interaction to initiate.

This precious time at birth is one opportunity you have to be a part of the awakening of your infant's mind. Making eye contact, talking in a soft voice, and touching your baby's body gently are universal behaviors that new mothers instinctively do in the first moments after birth, when they are given skin-to-skin contact with their babies in a warm, safe place. Feeling your own joy in this moment envelops your baby in an amazing dynamic of love. With the first opening of her eyes, touch of her skin, sounds, scents, and tastes, her brain begins to awaken and the billions of cells begin to interweave and connect. As soon as she comes into contact with the outside world and uses her senses, her brain begins to make the pathways and connections that will define her world and allow her to express who she is.

Birth is the first meeting between a mother and her new child. Although it is a monumental time, bonding with both parents is a process that unfolds over weeks and months. These tender, loving, and respectful interactions that take place will continue and deepen throughout infancy. As parents, when you care for your baby in a sensitive way, you are promoting healthy growth and development. Interacting in this way at

birth and beyond will also have an effect on you. These moments of amazing joy will help you to be open to an aspect of
yourself that will emerge, grow, and develop as you interact
with your baby. All of you are profoundly affected by the way
the others reach out. The whole family expands into a new
way of being when a baby arrives. This experience of bonding
brings out as much new information in your instinctual self
as it does in your baby. As you connect with your baby from

The magic of a new born person.

that gentle soft place, she will respond to your attention. As you both sink more deeply into this interaction, you may find that you are bringing each other into a new form of awareness through the bonding process. There is magic in those early moments that your family spends together.

Of course, we recognize that not every moment of early parenthood is magical; in fact, for most new parents, many of the moments can feel frustrating, tiresome, and mundane. You are in the midst of learning a whole new set of skills and getting to know a brand-new person. This can be very challenging at times. Still, it is important to do your best to try to savor the moments of connection between you and your baby. This early time is fleeting, yet it is a time when you are instrumental in your child's development, specifically her brain development. Do not underestimate it, this is important work. Do what you can to be present and available to your baby when she seeks connection with you, and give yourself a break when you start to feel overwhelmed and need to take some time to refill your cup and regain your own emotional balance. Parenting is a marathon, not a sprint. Doing your best to tune in to your baby and connect deeply and authentically when you can is a true gift to both of you.

Attachment and Emotional Regulation

Eye gazing is a way of seeing, knowing, and feeling love that will strengthen the bond with your baby. When you are able to settle into moments of connecting, you may notice that he goes in and out of being engaged with you. Sometimes he looks away or glazes over. Other times he makes strong eye contact and connects deeply.

During these moments of connection, follow his lead. Engage when he engages, allow him the freedom to disengage when he looks away, and then come back into connection when he attempts to reengage with you. This is important because although making eye contact with someone you love seems simple, for a new baby, it is a demanding physical and emotional task. He is learning to connect with you, and as he learns he is making massive new neural connections. When your baby looks away, he is integrating those new connections formed by his experience. When you respect his need for integration time, you are also helping him develop a healthy emotional balance.

One of the goals of parenting is to help your child establish and manage his emotions in a balanced and healthy way. Balance is a very important part of all living systems. In biology it is called homeostasis. For example, our bodies all need to maintain a particular range of temperature to be able to stay alive (98.6 degrees Fahrenheit is ideal). If we leave that range, there are many body mechanisms to help us return to "normal," such as sweating if we are too hot and shivering if we are too cold. There are checks and balances for body pH, heart rate, fluid balance, and other body systems, all of which help maintain a normal range during change.

A calm presence will help baby maintain emotional balance.

The same system works on the emotional level. Although your infant has a natural sense of flow between excitation and integration, he is not quite able to navigate these ups and down by himself. In order to develop strong pathways for emotional balance, your infant needs consistent and repeated experiences of finding his way through emotional ups and downs with your love and calming presence to guide him. When these pathways have been well worn over time, he will be able to handle the stresses of life on his own with ease and facility.

Parenting Realities

The living truth of your time with your baby is that there are many interruptions, from the outside world and also from your inside world. You have both recently been through the physically, emotionally, and perhaps spiritually life-changing experience of birth, and you are both in an environment that has its own cycle of demands and changes. The wonderful thing is that the essential nature of life is resilience. Going in and out of balance is a part of life, and when we acknowledge that, it can be a great learning experience rather than a detriment. As a parent, you are busy cooking, answering the phone, attending to your other children, and so on, and that's all a part of life. If you misread your baby's cues, or are occasionally distracted from her, you can return to sort it out. Your baby's system thrives on making many kinds of connections, including repairing problems with you.

Resting together.

Inner Cycles

When things get busy, you might find that you haven't settled and taken a breath with your baby for a while. Your baby is learning how to create his own inner cycles of activity, but it is imperative to his health that you take time to settle with him. This gives him a template for how to find the resting place for himself. It's so worthwhile to find those moments of uninterrupted time in which you can tune in. Eye gazing while he feeds has the same effect whether he receives nourishment from the breast or bottle. It builds positive pathways in his brain that reflect the feeling that life is love. His system needs this to be able to settle.

When the tension of a busy life starts to build up for your baby, he may find it harder to settle and may start to have stress symptoms, such as fussiness or an uncomfortable tummy. This is the perfect time to start the CALMS steps. Your ability to be with your baby in a calm and settled way in the face of stress helps him to regain emotional balance. Repeated experiences of going back and forth between smooth sailing and choppy waters allows your infant to develop emotional fluency in the face of stress and novelty. This resiliency is the true indicator of a secure attachment.

In summary, it is important to create time for deep connection with your baby. During those times, you are supporting healthy growth in your child's brain. In addition, when you are able to tune in to his cues of engagement and disengagement, you lay the foundation of his ability to manage new experiences and big emotions throughout life. The more you do this with him, the more he will be able to do it on his own.

When you are not able to tune in or be as present with him as you like, know that you will always have an opportunity to repair these moments with your child. The goal is not to be a perfect parent, but rather to be a present parent. Do your best and love your baby!

PART FOUR

When Things Don't Go as Planned

I don't think it's anybody's conscious fault, but I think that the medical world does not validate the emotional, the spiritual life of the mother and child, the reality of human values. They are so focused, as rightfully they should be, on the physical, but they neglect the other, and the other is very important. Birth is a heart-opening, human experience that needs to be honored and respected and have as little medical intervention as possible.

—BARBARA FINDEISEN, INTERVIEW,
WHAT BABIES WANT, THE MOVIE

In Part III we spoke of the ideal bonding situation of a gentle birth where the mother and baby are not separated and are given the time and privacy to discover each other gently and slowly. This may not have been what you and your baby experienced. So what happens when things don't go as expected? Your birth may have had some minor deviations from the plan, or you may have had an experience that was very different from what you were expecting. This may have left you feeling pain and disorientation, and your baby feeling overwhelmed and confused. Whatever your experience, our intention in this section is to offer information and basic support. Clearly we are not offering medical advice or therapy, and the information in this section is not intended to take the place of professional

Security is everything to a baby.

intervention. If you feel that your baby or you are struggling and need help, please consult your doctor or midwife for advice and referral.

When Things Don't Go as Planned

As mothers, we all want to have a dream birth, and yet many things can happen during this precious time that are not what mother or baby intended or wanted. Most women try to put those difficult parts of the birth aside and settle into the next all-consuming act of being a mother to an infant. This is more than a full-time job and doesn't leave much time for anything else, especially if there are other young ones at home. For some, it may be easy to forgive and forget a challenging birth experience, but for many of us, the memories and body sensations of the memories linger and become part of our daily fabric.

For some mothers, the birth memories can appear as an unexpected feeling, an image, a physical sensation, a negative thought or judgment, a flash of anger, a wish that things could have somehow been different, a sadness, or a sense of loss. Sometimes the memory of an event can be suppressed, and yet the feelings associated with the memory just appear without any real explanation. This can be very difficult for a new mother to manage. How does she deal with a feeling she can't even explain?

The father or birth partner is another important person in the birth circle. Partners also have a profound experience during the process of birth and may have feelings about how things happened and their role in the birth experience. In the event

Healing with CALMS

Some body sensations that are associated with the memory of an overwhelming birth experience might include but are not limited to: a sinking or buzzing stomach, tight heart, discomfort or pain in the vaginal area or around a cesarean scar, recurrent headaches, muscle tension, sensations of weakness in the arms or legs, and uneasy, vague feelings that something is wrong.

of a separation of mother and baby, often partners are the ones who accompany the newborn through the hospital routines. They can be empowered or estranged by the experiences they have during this odyssey. This is often separate from what the mother's experience may have been.

Both you and your partner had life changing experiences at the birth, so now let's consider your baby and what her experience might have been. The possibility that a baby can have an experience at birth is a new idea in our culture. We must remember that the baby is indeed awake and profoundly impacted by what happens to her. There is also a tendency to imagine that the baby had the same experience that the mother had. This is unlikely to be true.

Now that we know that the mother feels *her* experience and the baby feels *her* experience, it is understandable why things

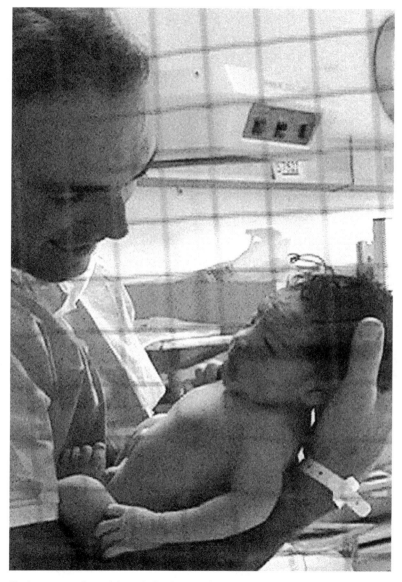

Fathers can play a big role in the newborn's life.

might be confusing. All of these feelings can seem overpower-
ing, and sometimes contribute to the overwhelming experience of the first weeks and months of being a new parent and
of being a new baby.

Life with a newborn demands that you "get it together." It
can be some time before you realize how much you and your
baby were impacted by the events of the birth. What happens
when things don't go the way you expected them to? What
if you see your baby and don't immediately feel love? What if
you are worried that your baby doesn't love you? You or your
baby, or both of you, may have had significantly overwhelming experiences before getting together. Although we cannot
provide all the answers, we can offer some guidelines about
how to work through these difficulties, should they arise. It
is very important to seek professional help if you have per-
sistent difficulties with bonding, breast-feeding, or any other
concerns.

Confusion

If you and your baby had any drugs, interventions, surgery,
separation, or an overwhelming and difficult labor and birth,
your first response to seeing your baby may be a heart full of
love and joy, or you may be feeling out of it and just struggling
to adjust. Sometimes people feel numb after an overwhelming
or traumatic event. You may ask yourself, "Why don't I feel
what I thought I would feel?" or "What am I supposed to be
feeling? What went wrong, why don't I feel anything?"

The Importance of Support

Some women have feelings of failure at birth. Although a woman will often take responsibility for what happens at the birth, sometimes it is the system that surrounds her that has failed her. We believe that most women, given the proper support during pregnancy and birth, are capable of having a birth that would satisfy and empower them.

Everyone has her own ways of interpreting an event. We cannot say that a particular experience will affect every person in the same way. Each of us is an individual, with very different coping skills. However, there are some common experiences that are likely to cause stress and can overwhelm both mother and baby. A person becomes overwhelmed when things happen faster than she is able to integrate them or when she cannot properly keep track of what is happening to her. At some point feelings of being overwhelmed become trauma.

Separation

One of the most common causes for your baby to feel overwhelmed at birth and in the early days of his life is to be separated from you. All mammalian babies, including human babies, have a strong and very primal instinct to stay with their mother.

Staying close is the one thing that is most likely to ensure survival and healthy development. It is stressful at the least, and in the worst case traumatic, for an infant to be separated from his mother. It also goes against the instinctive grain for the mother to be separated from her baby.

If you and your baby were separated at birth, the separation has become a part of your birth story that both of you will tell over and over again in your own way until you heal. You can use the CALMS steps to listen to your baby when he wants to tell that part of the story. You may be wondering how you will know when your baby is trying to tell you his version of the birth story. For example, if the separation was difficult for him, he may have a stronger need to be with

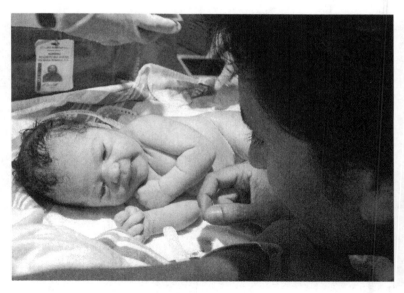

Keeping the continuity of contact and connection is meaningful to the baby and the parents.

you. He may tell you this by protesting when you try to put him down, hand him to someone else, or attempt to have him sleep away from you. In his first days and weeks, he will show his anxiety when you are separated. If you respond to him with lots of reassurance, holding, skin-to-skin contact, and touching, his need to be close will be honored, and this will help him heal. His anxiety about having been separated from you at such a critical time will be eased. This will also be beneficial when he is older and developmentally needs to separate.

Mother-baby separations are usually associated with other interventions. This is almost always the case for the baby. These interventions are sometimes necessary to save the life of the baby or mother, but also may be performed as part of a general protocol. They are all likely to impact both the mother and baby deeply. Standard interventions for mother and for baby include, but are not limited to:

- Induction of labor
- Rupture of membranes
- Restricted movement
- Medications and drugs
- Forceps
- Vacuum extraction
- Cesarean section
- Continuous monitoring

- Episiotomy

- Suctioning

- Resuscitation

- Separation

- Weighing

- Assessing

- Eye drops

- Blood draws

- Circumcision

We would like to reiterate that each person negotiates hardship and trauma based on several personal factors. What is devastating for one person may be challenging but manageable for another. The important thing is to consider your own experience and allow yourself to have your own feelings. It is also vital that you think about your baby's experience. Notice his behaviors, signals, and cues so that you can support him to express his feelings and be heard by you as well.

How Do We Sort This All Out?

One way to orient and find your way back to yourself, and into a deeper connection with your little one, is to use the CALMS steps. The CALMS steps are designed to help you be with and communicate with your baby under almost any circumstance.

Healing with CALMS

You may feel grief, loss, or despair over events that have passed. It is helpful to grieve properly over your loss if this happens. When you feel the emotions of the birth start to surface, take some time to lie down and see what your unconscious has to say. Stay with your emotions and body sensations even if they are unpleasant. Your body sensations are the key to your unconscious, where wounding is held. Feeling what happened at your baby's birth and allowing your feelings about it to come to the surface will help you get in touch with them. Whether you feel bad, angry, betrayed, hurt, teary, or maybe notice that you wish you had done it differently, feeling these feelings is part of the process will put you on the path to healing. The CALMS steps may be helpful in doing this. Be as accepting as you can of your feelings. Realize this is a reasonable response to your experience. Take a breath or maybe several slow deep breaths. If other emotions and experiences surface, allow those feelings as well. This is the way you heal, by allowing, acknowledging, and managing feelings with your breath. As they surface they become easier to manage with practice. If you find that you are consistently overwhelmed, seek help from a friend, your pastor, a therapist, or whatever support person feels right to you. No one should be expected to heal alone.

In this section, we focus on using CALMS to deal with challenging experiences at birth.

Using CALMS After a Challenging Birth

With a birth that didn't go as expected, feelings of having done something wrong, guilt, or blame can surface. This is a natural response. Many people who had a difficult birth spend some time feeling like they somehow just didn't do a good enough job, or that they failed.

Check In

The first step of CALMS is to check in with yourself. This means to be with what you are feeling in the moment—be it guilt, anger, shame, sadness, frustration, disappointment, or any other difficult feelings. This may be hard to do, but it is so helpful when you can just name your feelings. For example, it might seem nearly impossible to accept the feeling that you have failed or that you have done something wrong. Accepting your feelings rather than trying to get away from them is an important step in moving toward healing. It also helps your baby when you are able to separate what you are feeling from your feelings about her. Naming and owning your emotions helps to keep them from overwhelming your relationship with your precious, vulnerable baby.

Checking In

Elizabeth is the mother of seven-day-old Tobias. She and Tobias were separated at birth because the doctors were concerned about his breathing. After six hours, Tobias' breathing stabilized, and he was brought to his mother, but the separation was disorienting and upsetting for both of them. Now they are home, and Elizabeth is finding that every time she tries to put Tobias down to sleep, he startles awake and starts to cry. Elizabeth initiates the CALMS steps by checking in with herself and notices her anxiety rising. She wonders what's wrong with Tobias and fears she is doing something wrong. As she stays with herself, she notices that her heart feels constricted, and there is an edge of fear that something happened to her baby during the time they were separated.

Allow a Breath

Whatever you are feeling is valid. It is possible that the people around you don't fully understand what you have been through or realize that your birthing experience was a major life-shifting and disorienting event. Unfortunately, for moms and babies, people don't usually talk about the psychological impact of a difficult birth. You just went through an overwhelming experience and may still be trying to get your bearings.

The second step of CALMS is to allow a breath. Taking a breath can help you relax and settle in your body. When experiencing emotions involved with giving birth, it is important to be extremely kind and gentle with yourself. You have been through a very intense experience and are in need of sensitive

CALMS IN ACTION

Allowing a Breath

While holding Tobias, Elizabeth sits down, takes a breath, and visualizes her chest expanding around her heart. With each breath she attempts to slow down inside and take in more air. She acknowledges to herself that the birth was not what she wanted. A few tears roll down her cheek. Even though she is feeling sad, Elizabeth notices that as she acknowledges her own feelings, she is more able to shift her attention toward what her baby is feeling.

attention. In some cases, allowing a breath could be extended into getting a massage, speaking with a counselor, or taking time to sit quietly and grieve the loss of the experience you wish you could have had. Even though it may seem nearly impossible to do so, it is important to take some steps toward doing something that will help you come back to balance and feel good inside.

Listen

You cannot know what your baby's experience of birth was until you listen to him. In order to understand what is happening for your baby and how he is communicating, it is helpful to step outside of how you normally perceive your baby's actions. The way your baby acts, moves, and vocalizes is how he communicates his feelings and responses. Like you, sometimes his

---

CALMS IN ACTION

Listening

As she looks at her baby, Elizabeth remembers that just a few minutes earlier Tobias had fallen asleep at her breast. Knowing he was sound asleep she gently eased him down into his bassinet so that she could take a break. As soon as she carefully moved her hands away from his body he startled awake and began crying. Holding him she thinks about the alarmed look on his face and the way his body startled awake. As she thinks about his experience and how it is hard for him to settle unless he is lying with his chest on hers, the reality of what happened to him suddenly hits her. She realizes that that being separated from her is frightening to him. As the intensity of how that must be for him settles in, she wonders about his experience of the time when he was separated from her at birth.

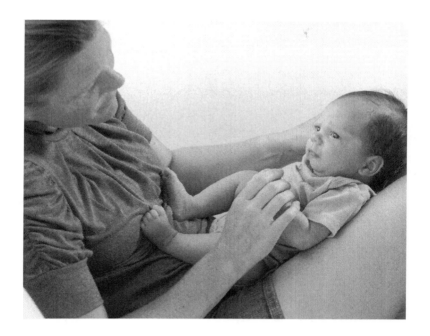

reactions are related to things happening in the present. And sometimes he is reacting to things that happened in the past.

The third step of CALMS is to listen. Once you have identified your feelings and owned them, you are more open and able to hear what your baby is telling you. Take a moment to slow down and shift your attention to your baby. View his movements, sounds, facial expressions, and body language as communication, and trust that he is trying to tell you something important about things that happened and how he feels about it. Your attention and willingness to listen communicates compassion and love, the sources of healing. What he needs is your physical and emotional attention.

Make Contact and Mirror Feelings

You want to acknowledge what you are seeing and feeling your baby express in the present moment. It is important to ac-knowledge that you understand that your baby might be trying to tell you about something from the past that had a big impact. Sometimes little things that happen in the present trigger feel-ings and sensations from past experiences. During these times she needs to know that you are trying to understand her and are there for her.

The fourth step of CALMS is to mirror your baby's feel-ings. This step communicates that you are listening and are trying to understand what she is saying. Your understanding is based on things like her movements, body language, sounds,

CALMS IN ACTION

Making Contact and Mirroring

Elizabeth looks down at Tobias and says, "Wow, my dar-ling, when I set you down you startled awake and began to cry. That alarmed look on your face made me think about what could cause you to be so afraid. I know how hard it was for me to be separated from you while we were in the hospital and wonder if you are telling me about that time. When you are in my arms you seem relaxed. I want to reassure you that we are together and that you are safe now."

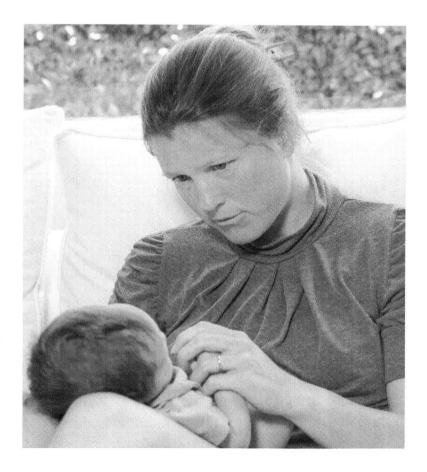

and facial expressions. Just simply let her know what you are seeing. In the case of our example, Elizabeth, the mother, put her baby down and saw how he startled awake as she took her hands away from him. She wondered about her time away from him because she was open to hearing and knowing what he was communicating.

Soothe

When there is some sort of trauma or overwhelming event that happens at birth, the baby may need extra time to process, integrate, and heal from what happened. The mother and father may also need extra care to process, integrate, and heal from

Soothing

Elizabeth held and talked to her baby the rest of the day. He slept and breast-fed contentedly until evening when his father, Peter, came home from work. Peter cooked leftovers from last night's dinner, while Elizabeth sat in the kitchen holding Tobias. As Tobias slept peacefully in her arms, they discussed her realization about the trauma of separation at birth. They decided to try keeping Tobias in their arms most of the time for at least the first six weeks of his life, noticing his cues until he seemed to be able to tolerate separation without fear. In order to support Elizabeth to be able to devote herself to Tobias' healing, they reached out to their friends and asked for help with meals and some housework. Tobias responded well to being closer to his mother. Over the next few weeks he began to relax and feel more comfortable. He startled less and over time was able to sleep better and be more adaptable to location.

what happened. It is unrealistic to expect the mother, who had her own trauma and struggle, to be able to heal herself and her baby without a lot of help and support.

The fifth step of CALMS is to soothe. In these situations, soothing takes on a new meaning because it must encompass the needs of the entire family. When there is a difficult or traumatic birth, the baby may need additional care, depending on his experience and your perception of his needs. The most effective way to help your baby come into balance and heal is to spend more time holding him; being held by his mother offers him the sense of security he needs and desires. He instinctively knows her body is a safe place. Helping your baby to heal his birth experience at an early age will make a difference for the rest of his life. It may seem like a big investment, but the benefits are profound.

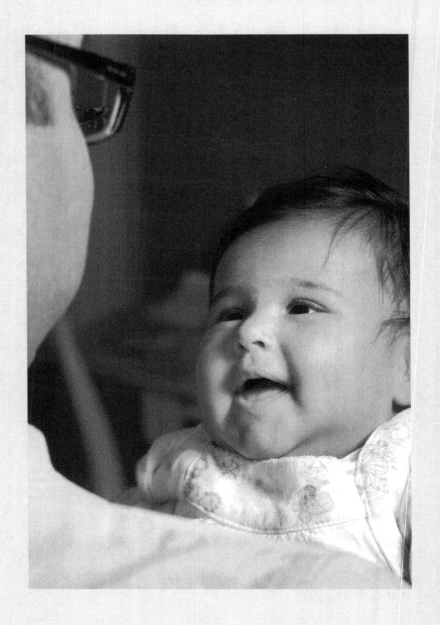

PART FIVE

Learning to Understand Your Baby

My friend has a baby. I'm recording all the noises he makes so later I can ask him what he meant.

—STEPHEN WRIGHT,
COMEDIAN, ACTOR AND WRITER

People often ask us how babies can understand what we say to them. Are they really listening? We think most parents have this curiosity about communication with babies. When Debby's first son was born nearly forty years ago, she tried to figure out if he was able to communicate with her as a newborn infant. She was never quite sure what all those wiggles meant, but felt very excited when she sensed that he was responding to what she was saying or doing.

Even though your newborn baby's brain is still developing, there is a person in there who wants to be seen and known. Although until recently we failed to register the person present in the infant, modern science is catching up with the sophistication of babies. We have many ways of measuring the awareness of infants, and now know that they care and are responding to what is happening to them and around them. Your baby has a strong drive to express herself. This inner drive is part of what propels her to focus on learning and developing. She wants to know that she is not alone in her experience, and she is doing everything she can to connect with you. She loves to hear your voice because she has been hearing it for nine months and it makes her feel safe. But how does she understand what you are saying?

Your Baby's First Steps of Understanding

What does your baby see and feel? Your baby's mind is wide open. All that is going on in his sphere of awareness is streaming into his brain by way of the senses. He is open to the full experience of the way you are connecting with him. He can understand your intention because he is taking in your entire approach to him as well as your words and the way you are saying them.

Your baby picks up the "music of language" as one of the first steps in understanding what you are saying. He interprets

Lots to say, but no words yet.

meaning through the sounds of your voice and your emphasis—
not necessarily by the specific definition of the words, but by
tone, intonation, force, and rhythm. The meaning behind the
words is carried by these dynamics. This is called prosody.

Body language is a nonverbal language we all converse in.
Gestures, pacing, breathing patterns, skin color, scent, heart
rate, and facial expression are forms of communication that
infants understand. It is a universal nonverbal language. Most
of nonverbal language is something we do and perceive un-
consciously. Since the intellectual cognitive part of your baby's
brain is still in the process of connecting up, he is perceiving
all of these communication cues with the part of his brain that
forms the unconscious. He does not filter the information the
way we do as adults but sees and hears all aspects of expression. What is really exciting is that he uses the same unconscious signals and body language cues that he recognizes and
understands from your body and voice to respond to you. It's
natural; he does it automatically, just as you do. The difference
is that your baby's mind is wide open to the cues, so he sees
and experiences your unconscious communication. Like most
adults, you may have suppressed your awareness of many of
these unconscious signals because you have learned to focus
primarily on words. That is why you don't always consciously
know what your baby is trying to tell you. The good news is
that you are still subliminally reading his body language and
hearing his voice tones; by opening your mind and your heart
to receive these subliminal cues, you can understand the essence of his communication.

While you are working to understand your baby's language, he is very intent on learning yours. Let's try to get a sense of his experience and just how hard he is working to learn to speak.

Your Baby's First Steps of Learning to Speak

Imagine being in a foreign country with no clothes, money, or food, and you do not understand the language. It immediately becomes clear that you must connect with the people in order to survive. They are friendly, welcoming, and seem to want to connect, but you haven't learned their language and customs yet, and they sometimes behave in unexpected and overwhelming ways. Are you safe with them? Can you trust them? How do you learn the language and develop connections? How do you let them know that you are scared, hungry, tired, sick, happy, lonely or sad? If you can't use words, do you think you could show them these emotions and needs? You might want to tell the story about how you got there. Is there any way you could do that before you learn to speak their language? What do they need to do to make the shift into being able to understand you? What could they do to help you feel understood?

Babies are in a similar situation after birth. They are newcomers to a new land and have a need to survive and express themselves, and they need to form a solid connection with their parents in order to live well. Like a foreign traveler, your new baby is in a place where the language has many complex pronunciations of sounds. She will develop new vocalization abilities by watching carefully and practicing intensively to master these new sounds.

Part of how she learns to speak is by watching the way you use the muscles of your throat, how you move your lips and tongue, and imitating how you do it. At first she does not have the coordination to be able to form sounds with her mouth and tongue. When she tries and practices, she develops the nerve pathways for those movements, and is able to do so. She has been studying your language since she was inside the womb. With this focus from early on and with constant listening, observing, and practicing, your baby is able to learn to speak. She has a purpose and intent, and is accomplishing a very high-level task. She is learning her first language and telling her own story at the same time. With time and patience you will learn her story.

Developing Gestures

Just as it takes practice to make words, your baby must practice to accomplish a coordinated movement to make a gesture. What we sometimes miss is that the intent is there from the start. Your baby is expressing himself in every move he makes. Even though his movements may be jerky or seem uncoordinated, his behavior is not haphazard or accidental. Fine-tuned motor skills are formed through the continuous intentional practicing of every movement. Although it may look like your baby is aimlessly waving his arms around, he is trying to move in a specific way that expresses his genuine intention, or expresses a response to the experience he is having.

Hand–eye coordination starts with an intention and is actualized by hours of practice.

Fine-tuning movement takes practice in the same way that it takes practice to throw a ball, play the piano, or thread a needle. Once you know that your baby is affected by everything that happens around him, you will begin to see that his behaviors and communications are organized, significant, and have a purpose.

What Parents Can Do to Understand

As much as we want to know how babies can understand what we are saying to them, perhaps an even bigger question is *How can I understand what my baby is saying to me?* As adults, we generally depend on words in order to ensure communication, but without words there are some other elements that we can focus on that are also very important in understanding your infant's communication.

This is a time when you can do the first two steps of CALMS and let go of excess thoughts and feelings. Are you thinking about all that you have to do today? Are you worried about whether or not you are doing this right? Are you multitasking? If you want to know what she is expressing, it is important that you be ready to receive that information from her. Focus your attention on receiving a communication from your baby, rather than working hard to figure it all out. Here are some things to consider as you tune into your baby:

- **Synchrony.** Come into synchrony and harmony with your baby. Settle in and get a sense of her mood.

- **Observation.** Notice the little details about how she is making eye contact and moving her body. Does she seem uncomfortable or relaxed? Notice what she is doing and try imagining what it is like to be a little baby; this will help you see and respond to her more clearly, and create large amounts of empathy.

- **Attention.** Become aware of the speed and placement of your attention. It is very helpful to your baby if you can stay in your own body and not project your attention into her space. Sometimes you can tell where your attention is by feeling what you are doing with your eyes. Are you focusing sharply or softly gazing from behind your eyes? Just relax your face and eyes and that will help you stay within yourself.

- **Pacing.** Observe your baby's pace. Notice her breath rate and the way she is moving her body. Is she rushing to catch up with you, or is she feeling settled and steady? Take a breath, and check in on your own pace. When you allow a breath, you begin to slow yourself down and are able to come into synchrony with your baby.

A Word About Pacing

We live in a fast-paced world and often need to attend to many things at once. As an adult you have learned to manage this rapid-fire input of sensory information. Your baby needs time to take in new information and assimilate it. It takes him much longer because these experiences are actually forming the neural pathways of his brain. He is imprinting his experience. If he is rushed, his pace will speed up, and he may begin to feel overwhelmed. A feeling of being overwhelmed creates neural pathways of flight or fight. When your baby is overwhelmed, he has to defend himself. He is no longer able to explore the world around him. One way he lets you know that he is overwhelmed and needs help is by crying.

While trying to interact with our very fast-paced world, babies may experience the world as moving too much too fast. Your baby's biggest job is to develop the millions of brain connections that will provide him with a map of his world. Part of this activity is to learn how to stay balanced when the environment is stimulating. When you allow a breath, you begin to slow your pace, and your baby can then catch up. When he has a calm internal state he can open to the world and continue to explore and develop. When you slow down, you automatically become receptive to your baby's voice and body language. Slowing your internal pace can open your mind to the reality of your baby's experience.

Bringing Unconscious Observations to the Surface

You and your baby are tuned into each other more than you are with other people. You know things about your baby because you are his parent. You are already receiving information from him in your unconscious mind and body in a detailed yet sophisticated way. We want to encourage you to believe what you know about your baby: believe your little guesses and intuitions, believe your inner voice and body instincts. These messages are coming from your unconscious understanding of your baby's cues. If you listen to your inner voice you will tune into that level of communication and will become even more conscious of what your baby is saying.

Communication Steps

Part of understanding your baby's communication is being able to recognize what is happening inside your little infant. What is she experiencing? The steps in the CALMS protocol remind you to stop, look, and listen, and then to mirror and soothe:

- **Listen.** Notice the little details about how she is making eye contact and moving her body. If she is working hard to stay balanced, she may furrow her brow, splay her fingers or have blotches of color on her face, or be unusually pale around the mouth or forehead. She might spit up, get the hiccups, or yawn a lot. These are all signs of nervous system effort, and it means she needs some help to come back into balance. If her hands are relaxed and folded together on the midline, or if she brings her hands to her mouth, she is helping herself to settle. If her brow is not furrowed or if she is relaxed and making eye contact, she is more balanced.

- **Mirror.** Notice your baby in greater detail than you usually do and imagine what she is experiencing. Make the facial expression or hand gesture she is making. What are you feeling when you do that? Let her know that you are interested in her, and reflect back to her what you see her doing and what you think she may be feeling.

- **Soothe.** If she continues to show signs of nervous system distress, or if she is falling apart and crying, you can help by gently making contact and speaking to her in a low, slow voice. Gently help to contain her movements if she is flailing. You can do this with your hands or with a blanket to lightly swaddle her. If she is showing the signs of overstimulation, try to reduce the amount of stimulation in the environment. Dim the lights, move to a quiet spot, and speak to her softly.

Communication Stories

Now that we've introduced you to these concepts we are going to put them into action. The following is an example of a communication that you may have had with a baby. We have added dialogue for the baby. These are our words and interpretations. Your baby will have her own intent and meaning. Our hope is that you will use this as a guide to listening and sensing what babies are saying.

This little one is looking at his mother and chewing on his fist. It seems that he is having a pleasurable experience. When he has absorbed all of the love and encouragement from his mother that he can, he looks down for a break so he can assimilate what he saw and felt.

Now he is looking down and has stopped chewing on his fist. This is his way of tuning out excess stimulation so he can focus inside and integrate his interaction with his mother.

You are visiting your friend and her baby. After greeting your friend, you sit down next to them and look at the baby. You smile and say, "Hello."

The baby looks at you for a moment, then smiles and quickly turns her face into her mother's body. For a baby this usually means, *"Hang on a sec, that was so exciting and full of stimulating information I need a short break to assimilate what just happened."*

Sure enough, the baby is soon looking back at you again full of expectation to see what you are going to do next. If your next move is to reach out to take the baby in your arms, you probably just went out of the baby's comfort range. The head turns again, and she clings to her mother's neck. *"Yikes! I wanted to play around with you, but I can't leave the safety of my mother! That's just too much for me!"*

If you pull back your energy and kindly acknowledge her response, "I'm sorry, that was too much too fast," she will reengage with you. *"Wow! Someone who understands me! Okay, I can risk with you because you are responsive to what I am experiencing."*

If you keep following her cues for her ability to take you in, you will soon reach a point where she is ready to try being held by you. But once in your arms, she may decide that wasn't such a good idea, and turn back to her mother. *"I thought this was going to be okay, but I'm actually not ready. My mistake. Get me out of here. Mommy!"*

If you acknowledge her desire to be with her mother and let her go back, you will have just gained some points as being trustworthy. *"Gee, she listened to me again. Let's see if she still wants to play peekaboo."*

If you make fun of the baby for being a mama's girl you might lose some points. *"Hmmmm that's embarrassing, not sure I really like this person. I am not going to look at her again. I think I'll pretend that my fist tastes really good now and see if she will play with someone else for a while."*

All of these body responses are classic infant communication actions; once you know what to look for, you will see babies doing this time after time. Watching a baby cycle through engaging and disengaging during any interaction can provide a good clue to her pacing needs and ability to handle the experience she is having.

Infants Are Living Up to Their Potential

Babies are highly motivated to learn. You have probably seen a baby try to master some skill until he accomplishes it and then further fine-tune it. Your baby wants to express himself and is doing his best to convey his feelings and responses. He may not have the tools to communicate it clearly, but he is working toward sending the message. Before he comes into a state of accomplishment, he already has the intention. First your baby conceptualizes the task, then his brain and body are stimulated to become capable of doing it. We frequently hear the saying, "Believe that you can do it and you can." Your baby models this every day.

Breaking the Ice

Listening and responding to your baby might be a new concept since taking babies' communications seriously is not yet the norm in our culture. Mostly people try to soothe the baby

Developing Attention Span

The social part of your baby's brain is growing and developing. She wants to practice interacting because it is through interaction that she makes continuous tiny adjustments in her ability to take in just the right amount of information. Your baby will give you cues about what her needs are for pacing and connection. She will use her body language, breathing rate, eye contact, and facial expressions to let you know when she starts to feel overwhelmed. Your response to her cues helps her to learn to regulate her feelings. It is through this ability to self-regulate that she is able to hold attention and to express herself. The more she fine-tunes the skill of sorting out her sensations during interaction, the longer she will be able to hold her attention with whom or what she is interacting. The neural networks that she is building while playing and interacting with you now are the foundation for how well she will be able to interact and hold her attention later.

and don't realize the possibilities for connection and mutual understanding.

So how do you get started? What do you look for? The first thing is to see whether your baby is ready to make contact with you or if he is overwhelmed and avoiding contact. Even if your baby is upset, he may still be reaching out for connection. If he seems very upset, he probably needs your help to get back to balance. The purpose of assessing your baby is to understand what your baby needs in order to feel safe and find a way to settle down.

Is your baby trying to make contact with you, or is he avoiding contact? Avoidance may mean that he is overwhelmed with too much sensory information. You can get your first clues by where your baby is looking. Is he making eye contact? Is he reaching out to touch you? Is he listening intently to your words (with or without eye contact)? Is he snuggling into your chest? These are all obvious ways to make contact, and can be done while your baby is smiling or crying. He doesn't have to be happy to be trying to connect with you. He can still be reaching out if he is upset. When your baby starts to go to the edge of being out of contact, he might avert his gaze, squint his eyes, and, if really upset, arch his back and cry with his eyes closed and his fists clenched. He might even flail his arms in an attempt to get your attention. If this is happening he has gone out of his range of ability to regulate himself and needs help to settle back down.

Now that you have determined if your baby is trying to connect or is in the midst of losing his emotional balance, you

Becoming a safe harbor.

are ready to find out more. Remember to do the first two steps of CALMS by checking in with yourself and allowing a breath before you investigate your baby's responses further. Whether your baby is crying and out of contact or ready to play, the next step is to let him know that you see him.

Now, we're going to look at two examples: one baby who is not out of connection but just having a hard moment. The other baby goes out of connection and then comes back in.

CALMS IN ACTION

Becoming a Safe Harbor

To help your baby rebalance, start the CALMS protocol. Now that you understand how much information is streaming into your baby's brain through the senses and how it affects your baby, you can more fully understand why it is important to settle your own system first. Your baby feels where you are and experiences what you are feeling inside, not just what you are saying with words. If you can get to the simple place of being just who you are in this moment, without judging yourself, or feeling guilty or distracted by outside worries, then there is less subtle information coming out of you. That makes it easier for your baby to settle down too. The first two steps of the CALMS protocol—checking in and allowing yourself a breath—will help you to become your baby's safe harbor.

Example 1. The baby is in contact with her mother, and the mother follows her cues.

In this scenario, the mother laid her three-week-old baby on the bed several minutes earlier so she could get dressed. We will describe what the baby is doing nonverbally and what we imagine the baby might be trying to say. Again we have made up a dialogue for the baby to give voice to her signals. Your baby is going to have her own voice and her own story. As you follow the CALMS protocol, you are developing your ability to hear what your baby is saying.

BABY: Looks a little cross and is starting to fuss. Voice is more fretful and out of sorts. *"What's going on here? I have been lying in this position for an eternity!"*

MOTHER: "Hi, sweetie, I hear you talking to me. It sounds like you might be starting to get irritable about something. What's happening for you?"

BABY: Makes eye contact, furrows brow, and wiggles uncomfortably, waving her arms in the general direction of her mother. *"I need to move my body but I can't seem to get this thing going. Where are my muscles? Pick me up!"*

MOTHER: "It looks like you want to move in a way that you can't do yet. Let me see what happens if I support your back. Here comes my hand to your back." She slides her hand under her back and gives her a slight side posture.

BABY: More wiggles and grunts as she tries to scoot her body along the bed, doing a kind of sidestroke wiggle. *"Okay, now we are talking. I can do a lot more with your support. This is hard work, but feels good."*

MOTHER: "Gosh, you really want to be able to move your body, don't you? Here let me give you some support on your feet." Her other hand gives her foot support, something she can push off of.

BABY: Big effort noises. Pushes reflexively against the foot support and turns over to belly as she scoots across the bed. *"That's just what I needed. Ho! Ho! Here we go. I know I am on to something now. This makes me feel strong."*

MOTHER: "Wow, you can really scoot! That was amazing!"

BABY: Bobbing head up and down on the bed, sticking out tongue. *"Oh wow! That was a workout. I am starving."*

MOTHER: "Hmmm that's a sign language I definitely know. I think you want the breast." She comes up next to her and they breastfeed with eye gazing.

BABY: Soft sounds. *"I feel really good."*

Example 2. The baby is out of contact, and the mother and father work together to help him find his way in.

In this scenario, the baby was born after an average, normal, natural birth. The nurse cleaned and wrapped the baby in a receiving blanket in the room with the mother and placed him on his mother's chest in a breast-feeding position. The baby is physically healthy but disoriented and agitated. The parents work to come into synchrony with the baby and respond to his cries.

BABY: Squirming and grimacing with short almost frantic outbursts. *"Whoa! Wait a minute! What's happening? Where am I?"*

MOTHER: "Oh my Gosh! My *baby!* You are so beautiful!" [Notice the mother's energy and excitement does not quite match what the baby is experiencing.]

BABY: Continuing to squirm and squawk, waving one arm around. *"Hey, help! I am all tangled up in this blanket and can't figure this out. What's happening?"*

MOTHER: "Hi, honey, what's the matter? You are really struggling."

BABY: Starting to really wind up into a frantic cry. *"Where is my mommy! Help!"* [When feelings of being overwhelmed set in, we lose track of what is around us. In this baby's experience he could only feel the disorientation of being wrapped and moved around randomly by the nurse. So far, his instinctual expectation of what should be happening is not being met, and he is becoming frightened.]

MOTHER, to her husband: "Honey, help me get this blanket off of him. I think we need to have skin-to-skin contact."

FATHER: "Hey, sweetheart, I am going to unwrap you from this blanket. You are all tangled up and need to feel mommy's skin."

BABY: Crying loudly. *"Uh-oh! I am getting lifted up! No! No! This is not a good thing! Help!"*

MOTHER: "Oh, honey, you are so upset. It's going to be okay." She looks to her husband. "Just get him back on my tummy. We can get the blankets off while he is lying on me."

FATHER, noticing he is getting anxious, stops himself and takes a deep breath: *"Okay, baby, we are here with you and just trying to get you sorted out."* He gets the blanket mostly off, and the baby goes skin-to-skin on his mother's belly.

BABY: Stops crying and makes some gasping, croaking sounds.

MOTHER: "That's better." Rubs her baby's back softly. "Okay, now, just get a breath here. You are on my tummy, and we are right here." Mother takes a deep soothing breath, and so do the dad, the doctor, and the nurse.

BABY: Breathing hard but not crying anymore. *"This is more like it. I'm definitely in the right place. I hear Mommy's voice, and I feel so close and warm. I needed this."*

MOTHER: "That's right, little one. Just take your time. You are here now, and you are safe."

BABY: Settling and breathing normally. Starting to move his head from side to side. *"Okay, here we go. I am ready for the next part of this. I think I need to find where the food is. There is something I need to do. I want to push with my feet."* Starts to push and scoot up to the mother's breast. Grunts and makes little smacking sounds. *"This is amazing. I feel so strong. I can do this. Here I go."*

MOTHER: "I see you pushing your way up to my breast. Here is my hand on your foot for some support. That's right. You are so strong." She looks at her husband. "Look at him. Isn't he amazing?"

BABY: Rooting and rubbing his cheeks against his mother and making more effort sounds, he finds the breast and latches on. *"This is it. I made it. This is going to be a good life."*

Listen to Your Baby's Story

Every baby is going to express himself and tell the story of his experiences and feelings in his own way. The examples in this book are just ways that other babies have told their stories.

They may not be exactly what your baby is doing. Please re-member to understand your baby from your gut and not from your head. The sounds and movements your baby makes are how she tells her story. We can give you some ideas about what these expressions mean, but you need to fill in the context. Trust yourself, and trust your baby.

PART SIX

Parenting Questions & Answers

We cannot prepare for the future without embracing the meaning and the relevance of the baby's perspective on life.

—MICHEL ODENT, M.D.,
OBSTETRICIAN, AUTHOR

We hope this book has opened your eyes to a new way of thinking about your baby and that you are feeling inspired to find your way toward creating a deep and connected lifelong relationship with your beautiful child.

The purpose of the CALMS method is to give you a way of "being with" yourself and your child, no matter what style of parenting you are using.

Now that you have read the book we are going to offer you a series of common questions and answers that parents have about using the CALMS method.

Checking in with myself does not come naturally.
Will I ever get the hang of it?

First and foremost, give yourself a break. For most of us this is a new skill. You might not get it right away. In fact, it might feel awkward and unnatural for a little while. Like learning any new skill, it takes time and patience, and a lot of self-love and appreciation.

Consider it like learning a new instrument. You have to practice before you become proficient, but the more you practice, the easier it will become. After a while, it will feel like second nature. One way to start honing the skill of checking in is to pick one or more times during the day when you consciously ask yourself, "How am I feeling? What sensations do I notice in my body?" You might do this when waking in the morning or as you are falling asleep at night. Another good time is when you sit down to nurse or feed your baby. Creating the habit of checking in with yourself takes time but is well worth the effort.

Sometimes when I check in with myself I don't
believe what I am sensing. How can I get to what
I'm really feeling?

When people are learning the step of checking in, it is common that they get a sense of something that they are feeling, and then doubt or deny it. It really helps to trust yourself and to trust your feelings even if they are uncomfortable. Just as when you are listening for your baby's feelings, it helps if you accept what comes up. If it's not what was expected, be honest and curious about it. If you are having trouble figuring out what you are feeling, ask yourself, "Am I feeling scared, angry, frustrated, disappointed, resentful?" Give yourself some choices and see which emotion resonates.

Sometimes when I check in with myself I realize that I am feeling angry and resentful. What do I do with those feelings?

Ask any parent and you will realize that you are not alone. These are normal feelings that tend to arise when we feel overwhelmed and stressed. Giving yourself time to calm down is way more beneficial to you and your baby than trying to parent from an angry or frustrated place.

During this time it's extra important to practice the second step of CALMS—allow a breath. This step is about doing whatever it takes to slow down and come back to the present moment. If the feelings of frustration and resentment are there, you can't just wish them away or step around them. Acknowledge what you are feeling, and do what you can to move through the emotions—take deep breaths, slowly drink a big glass of water, walk into another room, or go outside and get some fresh air. If you practice self-care and the feelings of frustration or anger continue to come, you may need more help. Be willing to ask for support from a friend or family member or possibly seek counseling.

I try taking breaths to center myself but it doesn't work. Is there something wrong with me?

Just like checking in with yourself, this may be a new skill. Be patient and practice often. Start becoming more aware of taking breaths when you are not particularly stressed. If you feel like breathing is not your best tool for calming yourself down right now, try to find other things that work better for you. More and more studies are pointing out that nature has a balancing effect on us. Find a view, a place outside, or even a house plant you can connect with. Another calming elixir is water. Drink it, splash it on your face, wash your hands, and take a shower or bath. There is no right way to slow yourself down; the key is to find what works for you.

I feel like there is no time to attend to myself first when my baby needs me because it feels wrong to let my baby cry even for a little while. How do I deal with that?

Of course it is difficult to hear your baby cry. It's completely natural and appropriate to want to attend to her needs as soon as she shows signs of being upset. What we are suggesting is that when you hear her cry, before you react, take a very brief pause to notice how you are feeling. This will allow you to slow down before attending to your baby. The first two steps of CALMS—checking in and allowing a breath—can be done in less than ten seconds. Taking just ten seconds to collect yourself before you attend to your baby will allow you and your baby to calm down sooner. Ultimately, you will have an easier time calming her down and she will spend far less time upset. Think of it as a small investment in everyone's long-term well-being.

The third step of CALMS is to listen. I listen but I still don't know what my baby is saying. Now what?

In the beginning, it is very normal to feel like you do not know what your baby is communicating. The point of listening to your baby in the early weeks and months is to communicate your presence, to allow your child to feel that you are interested in knowing him, and to try to understand what he is telling you. Be patient. You are getting to know this new person who speaks a different language and has a different story.

Over time you will learn what your baby is saying. And in doing so, you will have laid the foundation for a very healthy and trusting relationship.

What if I think I know what my baby is saying and I try to help him but it doesn't work? Can you address what happens if you incorrectly interpret what your baby is saying?

In the process of communication, misunderstandings are common. It's normal and happens to everybody. Remember that the listening and mirroring steps of CALMS are intended to be repeated. Think of this as a process of discovery. Just like in all relationships, you might not understand what your baby is trying to tell you all of the time. Do your best, try things, and trust that your baby will give you feedback on how you are doing. Even if your baby is still crying after you responded, you might not have been completely wrong. Watch your baby's shifting responses to your words and see if you can refine your understanding.

It is also possible that you may have perceived the communication clearly and your baby wants you to know more about his feelings. Keep listening. Keep reflecting. Try different things. Your baby is not looking for perfection, just connection.

There are times when I understand what my baby wants, but I can't do it right away. What can I do?

This will happen; you are human. During these times it's helpful if you can acknowledge that you understand that your baby wants something; then tell your baby what you are feeling or needing to do instead. For example, it might be obvious that your baby is ready to eat because she is rooting and starting to squawk and cry out. When you check in with yourself, you notice that you have to go to the bathroom. At this point it is better for you to take care of your own need first and then take care of your baby. You might say, "Dear one, I know you are hungry and ready to eat, but before I can feed you, I must go to the bathroom." Your baby will probably cry until you start to feed her. That's okay, especially if you or someone else is available to tell your baby that you understand she is hungry and ready to eat. When you return you can let your baby know that you really heard her and are ready to feed her for a good long while.

When my baby cries, all I can think of is what can I do to make him feel better. Why should I mirror his feelings when I can go straight to soothing?

When your baby feels upset, yes, he does want you to help him feel better, but before you offer soothing, he wants to know that you understand how he is feeling. Here's an example that will illustrate this point. Imagine you are really upset and you have a strong need to tell someone you love about what is happening. You go to your best friend for support. She takes one look at you, puts her arm around your shoulders and says, "Wow, I see that you are really sad, tell me all about it." This makes you cry even harder because you sense that she really wants to hear about what you are feeling. After a little while of her sitting with you calmly, you slow down enough to tell her why you are upset. She listens and assures you that she hears what you are telling her. Next, she offers you a glass of water. You drink the water and notice that you are feeling much better because you have been able to express your feelings to someone who was able to be present with you while you were upset.

Now, imagine the same scenario, but this time you go to a friend who is not quite so relaxed. You walk in crying, and she says, "Oh, you are going to be just fine. Here, have a drink. You're okay; don't worry about it." You sense that she does not really want to hear what you have to say. You might stop crying but it is likely that you will not feel settled by this friend's actions.

Which type of care would you prefer? Our point is that when your baby is upset he needs to feel that you are with him and that you are empathizing with his state before you try to move him beyond that experience. At times you may find that your baby won't let you soothe him. This is often a strong signal that he may need you to settle yourself more and listen to what he has to say.

I feel silly talking to my baby. How can I become more comfortable with it?

We understand that at first it might feel awkward or odd to talk to your baby, but the more you do it the easier it becomes. Eventually talking to your baby will feel natural.

It's important to tune in to your baby. When your baby is engaged with you, tell her about where you are going, what you are doing, and the things you are seeing. She will appreciate the contact. Even if she is not engaged, it is still courteous to give her the heads-up on what is happening around her, especially in the midst of transitions or when things are going to be done to her body. When she is relaxed, be mindful of slowing down and letting her have space to just be. Babies are often happy to have connection without a lot of words, especially when they are with the people they love. Trust that you will have a sense of when it's time to talk or when it's just time to be.

How do I get a conversation going with my baby?

The idea of having a conversation with a young baby may be new to most people. When your baby is in a quiet but awake state, hold him about twelve inches from your face, check in with yourself, take a few breaths and settle yourself. As you are doing this, start to notice what your baby may be experiencing. Next, say a few words about what is happening, and then relax, wait, and see what your baby does. Mirror back to your baby what you see or hear him doing. Again, pause, relax, and see what he expresses. When you let your baby know what you are hearing from him, your baby will respond to that. Be open! His communication may come in the form of a wiggle, an arm raise, a facial expression, or a sound. Just notice and say what you see. By noticing, you are having a conversation. Try it for three to five minutes at a time. Each time you do this you will get more insight into your baby's world.

If I've done the steps of CALMS, and I've tried to soothe my baby but she still won't stop crying. Am I doing something wrong?

Not necessarily. Because she doesn't have the brain structures and neural pathways to filter out excess input, she can get wound up and overwhelmed more easily than you can. Sometimes crying is an expression of *"I just have too much going on right now. Wah!"*

Whether she is overwhelmed, has a stomachache (and sometimes these go together), or just feels out of sorts, your baby needs to have you there while she is having her feelings. Obviously, it's important to check to see if your baby is hungry, wet, hot, cold, or physically uncomfortable. However, if there is no consoling her, stay with her, repeat the CALMS steps, and let her know that you are there for her. As you learn to do the CALMS steps in situations like these, you are giving your baby the support she needs.

Intellectually I understand that sometimes my baby needs to cry but there are times when I can't handle it. What should I do?

There will be times when you feel like you just don't have it in you to calm your baby down. If you have another adult with you, such as a partner or friend, let that person know you need a break. Give your helper a minute to transition, and let your baby know what is happening. If you are alone with your baby, tell him that you are having a tough time, put him somewhere safe, and take some steps to calm yourself down. Let him know what you are doing and when you will be back. Remember to tell your baby each step of the way what is happening. If you are getting overwhelmed regularly, get help.

There may be times when you and your baby need to change the scene. Put him in a carrier or the stroller, or just hold him and get out of the house. Getting out into nature is a great way to help you and your baby shift out of a very upset state. If you can't leave the house, you may run a bath or take some time to lay down on the bed with your baby. Yes, it's important to listen to your baby when he is upset and sometimes it's also important to help him shift by offering a change of scenery. If you think that your baby is sick or in pain, consult your doctor right away.

Conclusion

The CALMS Steps have come a long way from when we first conceived them. What started out to be a simple protocol for being with a crying baby has turned into a basic template to use in good times as well as in the more challenging times. People have adapted these steps to meet their family needs, keeping the basic premise of respectful communication at the center.

As parents, we all want to raise children who are independent, trusting, and trustworthy. From the very beginning, we start to do the things we think will mold the child in that direction, and very often we end up parenting as our parents did, even though we promised we wouldn't. The CALMS steps call for a new approach and one that is not always easy to follow. In the end, it requires that we make personal changes, work on healing our own wounds, and come into greater personal balance.

Independence in a child comes with time. In the natural way of things, it is appropriate for a child to start out dependent. Sometimes we are in such a hurry for our kids to demonstrate their independence that we forget to give them time to develop independence authentically from the center of their being, in small steps in the beginning of their lives. Every child has a strong inner drive to be herself, to stand on her own, and to speak her truth. It is the same inner drive that causes her to learn language and the motor skills to stand up and balance on her own two feet. For a truly independent child, the first step is to hold her close, give her every assurance of love and care, and meet her infantile needs. With this solid, loving foundation, she will gradually become more confident of her independence in her own time. It is up to you to follow her early cues for both dependence and independence. Fulfill her developmental needs, and then let go and watch her fly!

Much of the same can be said for trust. When we use the CALMS steps to connect with our children from the start, we show them trust in the most fundamental of ways. We show them that their needs have value and will be met most of the time. We show them that when they express themselves, we will be here to hear them, and when they are afraid or need help, we are here to support them. A child who has been welcomed warmly into the world by family and friends, and who has been met with love and respect, will have developed a core belief that the world is a good place. She will believe that she can do well and that life is beautiful.

You want your child to grow and develop into a child you can trust. We think that trustworthy children come from parents who trust and believe in them, parents who accept their children's communications as genuine, and who respond to them with heart. When your child starts out with a brain that has formed in the context of respect and connection, she will be trustworthy. At every challenging time of her development, you will find that you do not have to lose contact with her to be able to take charge of the next layer of life. You are in cooperation with each other, and developmental stages like the "terrible twos" and the teen years will take on new and amazing dimensions. You will find that your child's behavior is appropriate, and her independence is gratifying to you. When you maintain respectful communication with your child, you will respect each other, trust each other, and be trustworthy. You will find that you have established a life-long relationship based on love and mutual respect.

This is the greatest blessing one can have in life, and we wish for this amazing experience of parenting to be your experience as well.

Acknowledgments

This book would not have been possible without the love, support and encouragement from so many people.

We are particularly grateful to our teachers and mentors—Marti Glenn, Wendy Anne McCarty, Ray Castellino, David Chamberlain, William Emerson, Thomas Verny, Barbara Findeisen, John Chitty, Michael Shea, and so many other incredible people who have inspired us along the way.

To our friends and colleagues who read the manuscript and contributed suggestions—Erica Holten, Karen Strange, Bernadette Noll, Jodi Egerton, Noey Turk, Kai Takikawa, Sally Carricaburu, Annie Yakutis.

To the fabulous photographers and the families who appear in the photos. Their presence has deepened the meaning of our words. We would like to extend a special thanks to Kyla Hobbs-Darilek the talented photographer who generously gave us the very special cover shot of Carrie's friend Vera Nylund.

And to our designer, Kris Tobiassen, for making this book more beautiful than we could have imagined.

And to our family members for their love and support throughout the writing process, and the innumerable babies, children, and parents we have worked with who have shared their wisdom with us.

References

Part Two

Chamberlain, David. *The Mind of Your Newborn Baby.* Berkeley, CA: North Atlantic Books, 1998.

Klaus, Marshall and Phyllis Klaus. *Your Amazing Newborn.* Cambridge, MA: Perseus Books, 1999.

Lipton, Bruce. *The Biology of Belief: Unleashing the Power of Consciousness, Matter and Miracles.* Santa Rosa, CA: Mountain of Love/Elite Books, 2005.

McCarty, Wendy Anne. *Welcoming Consciousness: Supporting Babies' Wholeness From the Beginning of Life.* Goleta, CA: Wondrous Beginnings, 2004.

Somé, Sobonfu. *Welcoming Spirit Home: Ancient African Teachings to Celebrate Children and Community.* Novato, CA: New World Library, 1999.

Takikawa, Debby. DVD *What Babies Want.* Los Olivos, CA: Hanna Peace Works, 2004.

Verny, Thomas and John Kelly. *The Secret Life of the Unborn Child: How You Can Prepare Your Baby for a Happy Healthy, Life*. New York: Summit Books, 1981.

Part Three

Gerhardt, Sue. *Why Love Matters: How Affection Shapes a Babies Brain*. East Sussex, England: Brunner-Rutledge, 2004.

Grille, Robin. *Parenting For a Peaceful World*. Sydney, Australia: Longueville Media, 2005.

Karen, Robert. *Becoming Attached: Unfolding the Mystery of the Infant-Mother Bond and Its Impact on Later Life*. New York: Warner Books, 1994.

Klaus, Marshall, Joh Kennell, and Phyllis Klaus. *Bonding: Building the Foundation of Secure Attachment and Independence*. Reading, MA: Addison-Wesley Publishing Co., 1995.

LeDoux, Joseph. *The Emotional Brain: The Mysterious Underpinnings of Emotional Life*. New York, NY: Simon and Schuster, 1996.

Lewis, Thomas, Fari Amini, and Richard Lannon. *A General Theory of Love*. New York, NY: Random House, 2000.

Shea, Michael J. *Biodynamic Craniosacral Therapy,* Volume Two. Berkeley, CA: North Atlantic Books, 2007–2008.

Shore, Allan. *Affect Regulation and the Origins of the Self: The Neurobiology of Emotional Development*. Hillsdale, NJ: Lawrence Erlbaum Associates Inc., 1994.

Siegel, Daniel. *The Developing Mind: How Relationships and the Brain Interact to Shape Who We Are*. New York, NY: Guilford Press, 1999.

Siegel, Daniel and Mary Hartzell. *Parenting From the Inside Out: How a Deeper Self-Understanding Can Help You Raise Children Who Thrive*. New York, NY: J. P. Tarcher/Putnam, 2004.

Sunderland, Margot. *The Science of Parenting: Practical Guidance on Sleep, Crying, Play, and Building Emotional Well-Being for Life*. New York, NY: Doring Kindersley Publishing, 2006.

Part Four

Buckley, Sarah. *Gentle Birth, Gentle Mothering: A Doctor's Guide to Natural Childbirth and Gentle Early Parenting Choices.* Berkeley, CA: Celestial Arts, 2009.

Castillino, Raymond. "The Stress Matrix: Implications for Prenatal and Birth Therapy." *Journal of Prenatal & Perinatal Psychology & Health* 15, 1 (2000), 31–62.

Emerson, William. *Treating Birth Trauma During Infancy.* Dynamic Outcomes, Petaluma, CA: Emerson Training Seminars, 1996.

Levine, Peter A. *Waking the Tiger: The Innate Capacity to Transform Overwhelming Experiences.* Berkeley, CA: North Atlantic Books, 1997.

Shore, Allan. *Affect Regulation and the Origins of the Self: The Neurobiology of Emotional Development.* Hillsdale, NJ: Lawrence Erlbaum Associates Inc., 1994.

Part Five

Pearce, Joseph Chilton. *Magical Child: Rediscovering Nature's Plan for our Children.* New York, NY: Dutton, 1997.

Greenspan, Stanley I. *The Growth of the Mind: And the Endangered Origins of Intelligence.* Reading, MA: Addison-Wesley Pub., 1997.

Mehrabian, Albert, and Susan R. Ferris, "Inference of Attitudes from Nonverbal Communication in Two Channels." *Journal of Consulting Psychology* 31, 3 (1967): 248–252.

Mitchell, Rachel. L. C., Rebecca Elliott, Martin. Barry, Alan Crittenden, and Peter W. R. Woodruff. "The Neural Response to Emotional Prosody, as Revealed by Functional Magnetic Resonance Imaging." *Neuropsychologia* 41 (2003): 1410–1421.

Nugent, J. Kevin, Constance H. Keefer, Susan Minear, et al. *Understanding Newborn Behavior and Early Relationships: The Newborn Behavioral Observations Handbook.* Baltimore, MD: Paul H. Brookes Publishing Company, 2007.

Orlinsky, David E., and K. I. Howard, "Process and Outcome in Psychotherapy." In *Handbook of Psychotherapy and Behavior Change (3rd ed.)*, edited by Sol. Louis. Garfield and Allan E. Bergin, xx–xx. New York: Wiley, 1986.

Index

acknowledgment
  of baby's desire, by mother, 114–15
  of mother's feelings and sensations,
      10, 89, 92, 129
  of your baby, 6, 35–36, 96
anger, 81, 90, 129
Anna, xiv, 1, 3
anxiety
  of baby, 11, 14, 87
  of mother, 11, 48, 58, 67, 87, 91
attachment theory, 41

baby (baby's)
  ability to respond, learn and
      communicate, xiv, 41–42
  acknowledging your, 6, 35–36, 96,
      114–15
  anxiety of, 11, 14, 87
  arched back, 117
  arm waving, 120
  assumptions about, new
      understanding, 41–42
  assumptions about, traditional, 41
  birth, bonding experience of, 65, 67,
      69–71

birth, talking to baby before, 25
birth, transition after, 49, 51, 63
birth experience, 41, 45–46, 49, 51,
      65, 74, 79–82, 84
birth story, 86
as "blank slate," 40
blood drawn from, 88
blotches of color on face, 111
body contact, close, 34
body language, 5, 19, 28, 30, 95–96,
      104–5, 110, 116
body movement, 20, 26, 28, 35,
      95–96, 106, 108, 112, 125
body sensations at birth, 81–82
body tension, 20
bonding and instinctual responses,
      70–71
bonding attachment with both
      parents, 69
bonding attachment with mother, 63,
      65, 67
bones, growing, 30
brain development, 43, 54, 62–64,
      71, 116
breast, instinctive movement to, 51

breast *(cont.)*
  breast-feeding, 2, 28, 34, 51, 56,
      65–66, 76, 84, 121–22, 128
  breathing pattern, 91, 104, 124
  breathing rate, 116
  brow, furrowing of, 111, 120
  CALMS and healing birth trauma,
      88–99
  change of scene, wanting a, 136
  cheek rubbing, 124
  communicates what he/she wants, 4
  communication to affirm your, 6
  continuous monitoring of, 87
  crying, 2, 9, 19, 33, 112, 117, 119, 137
  cues for caregiver, 5, 25, 35, 49, 69,
      74, 77, 88, 98, 104, 114, 116,
      120, 138
  cues from caregiver, 45, 104
  cycles of engagement and
      disengagement, 76–77, 115
  digestion and anxiety, 14
  digestive pain, 30
  disorientation of, 80, 91–92, 122
  emotional and physical presence,
      needing mother's, 54
  emotional balance, loss of, 72–73, 117
  emotional intelligence, 54
  emotional regulation, 71–72
  expression, desire for self-, 102, 105
  eye contact and chewing on fist, 113
  eye contact with mother, 27–28, 31,
      69, 72, 76, 109, 111, 116–17, 120
  eye gazing, 70, 76, 121
  eyes, averted gaze of, 117
  eyes, squinting, 117
  eyes looking away and emotional
      balance, 72–73, 117
  face, alarmed look on, 94, 96
  face, hiding of, 28
  face, scrunching up, 26–27
  face in chest, burrowing, 30
  facial expressions, 19, 112, 116, 135

feedback from, 132
focusing inward and integrating
    interactions with mother, 113
gestures, 104, 106, 108, 112
hand-eye coordination, 107
healthy development and loving
    interactions, 4
hiccups, 111
hunger, 28, 43, 132, 135
independence of, 137
information filtering through mother,
    45, 104, 135–36
inner cycles of activity, 76–77
inner nature, expressing, 45
inner states of parents, understanding
    and mimicking the, 5, 16, 46
intention of, 106–7, 115
latch on reflex, 51, 124
laughter, 43
lips of, 17
listens to tone, intonation, force and
    rhythm of mother's voice, 104
look of expectation, 114
love, nurturing and respect supports
    brain and nervous system of, 63
mental well-being, building blocks
    for, 41
mirrors behavior and incorporates
    it, 54
mirrors calmness of mother, 36, 46
mothers feelings, tunes into, 16
motivation for learning, 115
music of language, picks up on, 102
nervous system, 35, 41, 46, 63, 111–12
neural networks, 116
overstimulation of, 112
overwhelmed, emotionally, 46, 80,
    85, 110, 116–17, 122–23, 135
pain or sickness, 136
physical abilities, 43
physical and emotional attention of
    mother, requires, 95

physical discomfort of, 135
physical helplessness of, 51–52
pushing away, 28, 35, 121, 124
recognition and self-worth, 22
reflexes of a baby mammal, 51, 85
regulatory system, mother acts as an
    external, 35
relaxed, 5, 14, 96, 98, 109, 111, 134
rooting reflex, 37, 51, 125, 132
routine changes, sensitivity towards, 1
safe, loved and respected, needing to
    feel, 22, 52
safe, secure and cared for, needing to
    feel, 4–5, 14, 37, 46, 48, 51–52,
    69, 99, 102, 117
safe and cared for, conveying that
    baby is, 42, 52
seeing themselves through the eyes of
    others, 30
self-worth, feeling of, 22, 59
separation at birth from mother,
    85–87
sickness and doctor, 136
skin-to-skin contact and
    strengthening of vital body
    systems, 52, 68–69, 87, 123
sleep, 15, 34, 37, 46, 56, 87, 91, 94,
    98, 128
sleep, struggle to, 1–2
smiling, 27, 43, 114, 117
sounds, 19–20, 31, 95–96, 105–6,
    123–25
squirming and grimacing, 122
stimulation, environmental, 46, 51,
    100, 110, 112
stimulation, tolerance level for, 46,
    112–13
stress symptoms of, 76
teeth, emerging, 30
throat, tight, 11
trust in the mother, 36
trustworthiness of, 138

understanding, first steps at, 102,
    104–5
upset and clenched fist, 117
vocalizations, developing, 105–6
wiggling, 101, 120–21, 135
yawning, 111
betrayal, 89
birth
    attendants, 65
    baby's body sensations of, 81–82
    baby's bonding experience of, 65, 67,
        69–71
    baby's experience of, 41, 45–46, 49,
        51, 65, 74, 79–82, 84
    baby's transition after, 49, 51, 63
    bonding and attachment at birth and
        beyond, 67, 69–71
    CALMS after a challenging birth, 90
    CALMS and babies experience of
        birth, 49, 51
    CALMS and healing the trauma of,
        82, 88–99
    mother-baby separation at, 85–89
    mother's emotions, 89
    mother separation from baby at, 82,
        84–88, 91, 98
    mother's experience of, 1, 63, 65,
        69–71, 74, 79–82, 84–85
    parents and experience of, 81–82
    partner, 81
    separation at, 82, 84–88, 91, 98
    as spiritually life-changing, 74
    story, 86
    talking to baby before, 25
blame, 90
blood drawing, 88
body systems, 44, 52, 72
body tension, 20
bonding and attachment
    about, 63, 65, 67
    baby's experience at birth, 67, 69–71
    at birth and beyond, 67, 69–71

bonding andattachment *(cont.)*
  in first year, 67
  mother's bonding and instinctual
      responses, 70–71
  of mother with baby, 63, 65, 67
  with parents, 69
  realities of, 74, 76–77
  regulation, 71–72, 74
bonding relationship, 67
bouncing, 2, 34, 49
brain cells, 62
brain development
  about, 43, 54, 61–64, 71, 116
  baby, inner cycles of, 76–77
  cognitive brain, 104
  love, nurturing and respect supports
      brain and nervous system of
      baby, 63
brain structure, 40, 44, 62, 135
breast-feeding, 2, 28, 34, 51, 56, 65–66,
    76, 84, 98, 121–22, 128
breathing. *See also* step 2: allow a breath
  to center doesn't work, 130
  deep, 13–16, 27, 69, 89, 123, 129
  rate of baby, 116

caesarean scar, 82
caesarean section, 65, 87
calming elixir. *See* water drinking
CALMS
  about, 39–43
  after a challenging birth, 90
  babies, sorting out feelings, 48–49
  babies, what do they want?, 51–52
  babies are people, 43–44
  babies are sensing beings, 45–46
  babies experience of birth, 49, 51
  babies sense their feelings from
      caregivers, 46, 48
  baby, acknowledging your, 6, 35–36,
      96, 114–15
  baby's developing mind, 54, 56
  community support, 58–59

  crying baby and, 135–36
  example of mother using, 120–21
  feelings of frustration, what you can
      do for, 56
  healing birth trauma with, 82, 88–99
  nature and nurture, 44–45
  parenting journey, your, 3–4
  safety first, 5–6
  shushing to listening, shifting from, 4
  sorting things out with, 88, 90
  step 1: check in with yourself, xiv,
      9–11, 33, 48–49, 90–91, 109,
      128–29, 132, 135
  step 2: allow a breath, xiv, 13–17,
      92–93, 109–10, 128–29
  step 3: listen to your baby, xiv, 19–23,
      25, 33, 86, 124–25, 136
  step 4: make contact and mirror
      feelings, xiv, 25–31, 86, 96–97,
      122–23
  step 5: soothe your baby, xiv, 2, 16,
      33–37, 55, 98–99, 112, 116–17,
      135–36
circumcision, 88
communication
  breaking the ice, 116–17
  mother's, to affirm your baby, 6
  mother's, to convey safety and care to
      baby, 42, 52
  open-ended, 26
  steps, 111–12
  stories, 112–15
  unconscious, by mother to her baby,
      104, 110–11
community support, 58––59
compassion, 95
confusion, mother-baby, 84–85
coping skills, 58, 85
counselor/counseling, 93, 129

deep connection with baby, 76
despair, 33, 89
diapering, 5

difficult feelings, 48, 90
digestive pain, 30
disappointment, 90, 129
disorientation, 80, 91–92, 122
doctor, 65, 81, 136
doula, 65
drugs, 84, 87

Elizabeth, 91–92, 94, 96–98
embryology, 41
emotional (emotionally)
  balance, baby's averted eye contact
    and loss of, 72–73, 117
  balance, calming presence of mother
    helps maintain baby's, 72–74
  intelligence of baby, 54
  overwhelmed, baby's feeling of being,
    46, 80, 85, 110, 116–17, 122–23,
    135
  overwhelmed, mother's feeling of
    being, 9–10, 31, 71, 89, 129, 136
  presence of mother, baby needs, 54
  regulation of baby, 71–72
"emotional volume," mother's, 16
empathy, 14, 28, 61, 109, 134
environment (environmental)
  baby explores, 46
  demands and changes, 74
  influence in development, 44–45,
    62–63
  stimulation, 46, 51, 100, 110, 112
episiotomy, 88
eye (eyes)
  averted gaze of, 117
  baby seeing themselves through the
    eyes of others, 30
  contact and chewing on fist, 113
  contact by parents, 109
  contact with baby by mother, 27–28,
    45, 64, 69, 71–72, 109
  drops, 88
  gazing, 70, 76, 121
  hand-eye coordination, 107

looking away and emotional balance,
    72–73, 117
squinting, 117

fathers, 31, 81–83, 122–23
feeding, 5, 35, 132. *See also* breast-
    feeding
Findeisen, Barbara, 79
first trimester, 54
forceps, 87
frustration, 9, 11, 27, 33, 45, 56, 58, 67,
    71, 90, 129

genetics, 44
gestation, 45, 54, 62
grief, 89
guilt, 9, 90, 119
gut feeling, 46

harmony, 108
healing the trauma of birth, 82, 88–99
heart
  connection, 67
  rate, x, 72, 104
holding of baby, 17, 34, 92, 94, 98–99
homeostasis, 72
human development, xiv, 41, 44
hunger, 43

induction of labor, 87
inner
  cycles of baby, 76–77
  nature of baby, 45
  states of parents, mimicking, 5, 16, 46
  voice, 4, 20, 111
instinct (instinctive, instinctual)
  mother needing to trust her
    parenting, 4, 35
  movement to breast, baby's, 51
  primal, 85
  responses and bonding, mother's,
    70–71
  for survival, 51

intention
   of baby, 106–7, 115
   of mother, 102
"in the moment," 13, 31, 90
intonation of voice, 104
intuition, 20, 46, 111

Joshua (baby), xiv, 1
joy, 47, 65, 67, 69–70, 84

kisses, 55

latch on reflex, 51, 124
lifelong
   development continuum, 41
   physical and psychological health, 41
   relationship with child, 127
lips, 17, 106
loneliness, 105
loss, mother's sense of, 81, 89, 93
love towards baby, 10, 22, 30, 52, 58,
      63, 65, 67, 69, 74, 76–77, 84, 95,
      102, 113, 137–39

massage, 52, 93
medical intervention, 65, 79–81, 84, 87
midwives, 65, 81
Mike, xiv, 1, 3
mother
   acknowledging your baby, 6, 35–36,
      96
   acknowledging your baby's desire,
      114–15
   acknowledging your feelings and
      sensations, 10, 89, 92, 129
   anger, feeling of, 81, 90, 129
   anxiety, feelings of, 11, 48, 58, 67,
      87, 91
   baby's cues, responding to, 5, 25, 35,
      49, 69, 74, 77, 88, 98, 104, 114,
      116, 120, 138
   betrayal, feelings of, 89
   birth as spiritually life-changing, 74

birth emotions, 89
birth experience, 1, 63, 65, 69–71, 74,
      79–82, 84–85
birth trauma, CALMS and healing
      the, 82, 88–99
blame, feelings of, 90
body sensations, paying attention to,
      10, 89
bonding and instinctual responses,
      70–71
bonding attachment with baby, 63,
      65, 67
calming presence helps maintain
      baby's emotional balance, 72–74
calming response of baby, activating
      the, 36
calming your baby by turning
      inward, 14
checking in, feelings identified when,
      9, 48
communication with baby,
      unconscious, 104, 110–11
confidence, losing, 2
cues, subliminal/unconscious, 104,
      111
cues from caregiver, 45, 104
cues given to the baby by the, 45, 104
cues of baby, taking, 49
deep connection with baby, 76
despair, feelings of, 33, 89
difficult feelings, 48, 90
disappointment, feelings of, 90, 129
emotions, naming and owning your,
      9, 90
exhaustion of, 2
expressions of, 26
eye contact with baby, 27–28, 45, 64,
      69, 71–72, 109
face, baby looks at mother's, 51
failure, feelings of, 85
"failure as a mother" feelings of, 11
feelings, accepting and naming
      your, 90

feelings, making of, 49
frustration, feelings of, 9, 11, 27, 33,
    45, 56, 58, 67, 71, 90, 129
grief over experiences missed, 93
guilt, feelings of, 9, 90, 119
headaches, recurrent, 82
heart connection with baby, 67
holding baby offers sense of security,
    17, 34, 92, 94, 98–99
inner voice, listening to your,
    4, 20, 111
intention of, 102
intuition of, 20, 46, 111
lifelong relationship with child, 127
listening and focusing on baby, 21
listening and mirroring, cycling
    through, 26, 32
loneliness, feelings of, 105
loss, sense of, 81, 89, 93
love towards baby, 10, 22, 30, 52, 58,
    63, 65, 67, 69, 74, 76–77, 84, 95,
    102, 113, 137–39
medical intervention, 65, 79–81,
    84, 87
mirror back what you see or hear your
    baby doing, 135
mirroring baby's expressions, 27, 112
muscle tension, 82
napping with baby, 56
negative judgments of, 81
open mind, listen and watch with
    an, 20
overwhelmed, feeling emotionally,
    9–10, 31, 71, 89, 129, 136
parenting instincts, trusting your,
    4, 35
personal needs, taking care of your,
    132
reassuring baby, 87
relaxing and breathing, 56, 92
relaxing your body and mind, 5,
    48, 135
resentment, feelings of, 129

scent of, 51, 69, 104
separation at birth from baby, 82,
    84–88, 91, 98
shame, feelings of, 90
soft voice, speaking with, 69, 112,
    122–23
subliminal cues sensed with an open
    mind and heart, 104
talking with baby about what you see,
    27–28
throat, muscles of your, 2, 106
trusting your baby, 35
trusting yourself and your baby, 125
trusting yourself and your feelings,
    128–29
vaginal pain or discomfort, 82
validation of baby's feelings, 30
verbal communication helps baby feel
    safe and cared for, 42, 52
visualization exercises, 15, 92
water drinking, benefits of, 3, 14,
    129–30, 133
mother-infant connection, 65
music of language, 102

nature, 5, 44–45, 48, 74, 128,
    130, 136
negative thoughts and judgments by
    mother, 81
nerve pathways, 106
nervous system, 35, 41, 46, 63, 111–12
neurobiology, 41
neurological map, 54
nonverbal language, 104
numbness from traumatic event, 84
nurses, 65
nurture, 44–45

Ordent, Michael, 127
overstimulation of baby, 112
overwhelmed
    baby as emotionally, 46, 80, 85, 110,
        116–17, 122–23, 135

overwhelmed *(cont.)*
   mother as emotionally, 9–10, 31, 71,
      89, 129, 136
   parents as emotionally, 3
owning your emotions, 90

parenthood, 58, 71
parenting
   experience of, 139
   as a marathon, 71
   model of our parents, 137
   questions, 3
   realities, 74
   resources, 56
   role to help child manage emotions,
      72
parenting Q&A's
   about, 127
   breathing to center doesn't work, 130
   CALMS but the baby keeps crying,
      135–36
   checking in, developing the skill of,
      128
   checking in and finding anger and
      resentment, 129
   checking in and trusting my feelings,
      128–29
   conversation with a baby, how to start
      a, 134–35
   listening and mirroring the baby,
      20, 108–9, 131–32
   listening but what is the baby saying?,
      131
   mirroring baby's feeling and soothing,
      35, 133–34
   mother's needs *vs.* baby's needs, 132
   talking to my baby feels silly, 134
   time for a break, 136
   time for myself *vs.* crying baby, 130
parents
   attention, becoming aware of speed
      and placement of your, 109

birth experience, 81–82
calming presence helps maintain
      baby's emotional balance, 72–74
coping skills, 58, 85
inner voice, listening to your, 4
instinctive abilities, 4, 35
observing baby and making eye
      contact, 109
overwhelmed, feeling, 3
pace, adjusting your, 110
pace, observe the baby's, 109
sleep deprivation, 2
synchrony and harmony with baby,
      getting in, 108
past experiences, 96
Pearce, Joseph Chilton, 54, 61
physical
   abilities of baby, 43–45
   attention of the mother, baby requires
      emotional and, 54, 95
   body, child's, 62
   comfort of baby, 5
   contact from adults, 14
   contact from mother, 25
   development, child's, 62
   discomfort of baby, 135
   discomfort of mother under stress, 10
   helplessness of baby, 51–52
   lifelong health, psychological and, 41
   movement of baby, 35
   presence, 52, 54
   safety of baby, feelings of, 48
   sensations of birth, 81
   state of baby connected to internal
      volume knob, 16
   task, demanding, 72
   touch, 52
   well-being of baby, 3, 43
prenatal psychology, 41
present moment, 36, 128
primal instinct, 85
professional help, 80–81, 84

reassurance for baby, 87
references, 143–46
relaxation
    of baby, 5, 14, 96, 98, 109, 111, 134
    of mother, 5, 48, 56, 92, 135
resentment, 129
resuscitation, 88
rhythm of mother's voice, 104
rooting reflex of baby, 37, 51, 125, 132
ruptured membranes, 87

sadness, 2, 9–10, 81, 90, 92, 105, 133
scent of mother, 51, 69, 104
self-care, 13–16, 19, 34, 129
self-love, 128
self-regulation, 116
self-talk, positive, 14, 17
self-worth, 22, 59
separation at birth, 82, 84–88, 91, 98
shame, 90
sleep deprivation, 2
sleep-deprived, 56, 58
sling carry, 2, 34
soft voice of mother, 69, 112, 122–23
soothing techniques
    bouncing, 2, 34
    breast-feeding, 2, 34
    "emotional volume," turning down
        your, 16
    food, 6
    holding, 17, 34, 87, 92, 94, 98–99
    play, 6
    reassurance, 87
    rocking, 6, 34
    skin-to-skin contact, 52, 68–69,
        87, 123
    sling carry, 2, 34
    sweet sounds such as poems or
        songs, 34
    touching, 87
    walk in fresh air, 34
    white noise, 34

sounds, baby's, 19–20, 31
sperm and egg, 61–62
step 1: check in with yourself, xiv
    checking in, example of, 111
    checking in, how to, 9–10
    checking in, why, 10
    unplanned situations, 90–91
step 2: allow a breath, xiv
    breath, example of allowing a, 17
    breath, how to allow a, 13–14
    breath, why allow a, 16–17
    self-care, ways to practice, 14–16
    in unplanned situations, 92–93
step 3: listen to your baby, xiv
    about, xiv, 19–23, 25, 33, 86, 124–25,
        136
    listen, example of how to, 21
    listen, how to, 20
    listen, why, 21
step 4: make contact and mirror
        feelings, xiv
    baby mirrors behavior and
        incorporates it, 54
    baby mirrors calmness of mother,
        36, 46
    example of, 30
    how to, 25–30
    listening and mirroring the baby, 20,
        26, 32, 108–9, 131–32, 135
    mirroring baby's expressions, 27, 112
    mirroring baby's feeling and soothing,
        35, 133–34
    in unplanned situations, 96–97
    why do it, 30
step 5: soothe your baby, xiv
    about, 30–31
    soothe, example of how to, 37
    soothe, how to, 34–35
    soothe, why, 35–36
stimulation
    baby's tolerance level for, 46, 112–13
    environmental, 46, 51, 100, 110, 112

stimulation *(cont.)*
  overstimulation of baby, 112
Stone, Elizabeth, 1
stress symptoms of baby, 76
sucking reflex, 51
suctioning, 88
surgery, 84

teen years, 138
therapist, 89
Tobias (baby), 91–92, 94, 96, 98
trust
  baby's, in his/her mother, 36
  CALMS and connecting with our
    children, 138
  mother's, in her baby, 35, 125
  parental instincts, 4, 35
  in your child, 138–39
  yourself and your baby, 125, 128

unconscious communication by mother,
    104, 110–11
understanding your baby
  about, 101–2
  attention span, baby's developing, 116
  baby is out of contact and parents
    provide direction, 122–24
  baby's first steps at understanding,
    102, 104–5
  baby's first steps learning to speak,
    105–6
  baby's gestures, 104, 106, 108, 112
  baby's story, listening to your, 124–25
  CALMS protocol, example of mother
    using, 120–21
  communication and breaking the ice,
    116–17
  communication steps, 111–12
  communication stories, 112–15

infants live up to their potential, 115
mother as a safe harbor, 119
pacing, a word about, 109–10
parents, what they can do to
    understand, 108–9
unconscious observations, surfacing,
    110–11
universal behaviors, 69
universal nonverbal language, 104
unplanned situations
  about, 79–81
  CALMS, healing with, 82, 88–89
  CALMS after a challenging birth, 90
  CALMS and sorting things out,
    88, 90
  confusion, mother-baby, 84–85
  separation at birth, mother-baby,
    85–89
  standard interventions for mother and
    baby, 87–88
  step 1: check in with yourself, 90–91
  step 2: allow a breath, 92–93
  step 3: listen to your baby, 94–95
  step 4: make contact and mirror
    feelings, 96–97
  step 5: soothe your baby, 98–99
  support, importance of, 85
  when things don't go as planned,
    81–82, 84

vacuum extraction, 87
vaginal pain or discomfort, 82
validation of baby, 30
vocalization, baby's, 105–6

water drinking, 3, 14, 129–30, 133
What Babies Want (film version), 54, 143
Wright, Stephen, 101
Wyle, Noah, xiii, 39

About the Authors

PHOTO © EMILY PAYNE

Debby Takikawa, DC, is a well-known family chiropractor and director of the documentary film, *What Babies Want*. After seeing the amazing healing responses the audiences have to the film, Debby responded by writing this book. Debby recently developed the BABY International Film Festival, to give greater public exposure to the best films made about pregnancy, birth, breastfeeding, and early childhood. Debby lives with her extended family on an organic flower and vegetable farm in California.

For more about the *What Babies Want* book and film please visit www.whatbabieswant.com. To learn more about the BABY International Film Festival, visit www.babyff.com

Carrie Contey, PhD, is the co-founder of Slow Family Living and a nationally recognized early parenting coach, consultant, speaker, educator and author. Her passion is providing parents with the support, information, inspiration and tools to create conscious, connected and

PHOTO © LEON ALESI

balanced lives in all stages of family life. She earned her PhD in clinical psychology with a specialty in prenatal and perinatal psychology from Santa Barbara Graduate Institute. Carrie served on the board of directors of the Association of Prenatal and Perinatal Psychology and Health. She lives, works, and plays in Austin, Texas. To learn more about Carrie and her work, please visit www.earlyparenting.com and www.slowfamilyliving.com.

Photo Credits

page	photgrapher	page	photgrapher
xvi	Fran Collin	66	Fran Collin
8	Fran Collin	68	Fran Collin
12	Debby Takikawa	70	Judith Halek
15	Fran Collin	73	Fran Collin
18	Debby Takikawa	75	Fran Collin
21	Fran Collin	78	Fran Collin
24	Fran Collin	80	Fran Collin
29	Fran Collin	83	Debby Takikawa
32	Fran Collin	88	Judith Halek
38	Fran Collin	91	Fran Collin
40	Judith Halek	93	Fran Collin
42	Debby Takikawa	95	Fran Collin
47	Fran Collin	97	Fran Collin
50	Suzanne Arms	99	Fran Collin
53	Fran Collin	100	Fran Collin
55	Fran Collin	103	Judith Halek
57	Fran Collin	107	Fran Collin
59	Shu Takikawa	113	Debby Takikawa
60	Fran Collin	118	Fran Collin
64	Judith Halek	126	Debby Takikawa

About the Photographer

Fran Collin is an advertising, editorial, and fine art photographer. His work is published and shown internationally. We are so grateful for his constant commitment to the photos in this book and for his sensitive view of mothers, fathers, and babies. Fran and his wife, Denise, have a daughter Sofia. www.francollin.com; www.work-for-food.com

C

STEP 1
Check in with yourself

A

STEP 2
Allow a breath

L

STEP 3
Listen to your baby

M

STEP 4
Make contact and mirror feelings

S

STEP 5
Soothe your baby